FRONT COVER Aleppo Syria 1930s Stamp

BACK COVER Aleppo Baron Hotel.

ISBN-979-8-218-20009-1

simonechoueke@gmail.com

My Aleppo Sephardic Family & Our Friends

Simone Choueke

In Memory of my beloved parents Ezra and Lucie Chouéké
Sister Frieda Choueke Saadeh
Grandmothers Farida Chouéké and Setto Esses
Uncle Rafoul Esses
Nieces Nicole Saadeh Lieban and Lisa Choueke Blank
Renee Hazan, Grace Sassoon and all the
cherished departed friends and family members

TABLE OF CONTENTS

PART THREE

About Us

PREFACE

My name is Simone Choueke. I am the daughter of Ezra and Lucie Chouéké of Aleppo, Syria and Kobe, Japan. I feel privileged to belong to the Aleppo Sephardic community and to have been born to my kind and generous parents who gave me such a good life.

Ezra Chouéké went to Japan in the mid-1930s to export the imported textiles he was selling at a store in Aleppo. He returned to Aleppo to marry Lucie Esses, the daughter of Setto (Chammah) and the late Simontob Esses. They married on November 11, 1936. Birthdays were seldom recorded in Syria so Lucie chose her wedding anniversary date for her "late winter 1919" birth. She had just turned seventeen, Ezra was thirty-four. Together with Ezra's sixty year old mother, Farida (Chouéké) Chouéké, they arrived in Kobe in January 1937, and never left. Very soon after they established their household, Ezra's hospitality, Farida's famous cuisine and Lucie's youth and beauty made their home a center of the Middle Eastern community. Farida was buried in Kobe in 1957, and Ezra in 1991. Lucie remained physically healthy and lucid in her landmark house until she passed away a few days shy of her official 2019 birthday. I am the second of Ezra and Lucie's four children.

Why did I write this book? It is an effort to immortalize the members of my family and our Aleppo friends who lived with us or visited us in Japan. The splendid folk who came mostly from Spain, Portugal and Italy to live in Aleppo, this exceptional city, for some four and a half centuries. What is so splendid about us? First and foremost, we like ourselves and each other. We enjoy being together. Wit and beauty are traits we revere. Our sense of humor makes us cheerful and fun loving. We are happy, sociable, giving, and charitable. Of course, if we didn't have faults, we wouldn't be human. But those will not be covered here. My intention is to celebrate us.

What qualifies me to write about us? Obviously, I knew my grandmothers, parents, uncles and siblings. Growing up in Japan, I can only say that I don't remember a single dinner or weekend lunch when we did not have one or more guests at our table. They literally came from all over: New York, New Jersey, Florida, California, Hawaii, Canada, Cuba, Puerto Rico, Mexico, Panama, Columbia, Venezuela, Curaçao, Argentina, Brazil, Chile, England, Italy, France, Switzerland, The Netherlands, Egypt, Lebanon, Greece, Turkey, Israel, Iraq, Iran, India, Thailand, the Philippines, Taipei, Korea, Hong Kong, Australia…. Some stayed with us—for days, for weeks, a few for months; and one for more than a year. Most were on buying trips during the American occupation and the post-war boom; many were or became our father's customers. Later, as the businessmen passed through on their way to less expensive Asian manufacturing hubs, the tourists started arriving to sightsee and to buy pearls. The great majority of these visitors were our Syrians and the first stop for everyone was our house. The talk centered on who was where, doing what, married to whom. Since our grandmother only spoke Arabic and our father preferred his native tongue, my sister and I were able to follow the conversations and eventually make the connections among those mentioned—the individuals and the families that constituted our tribe.

Frieda and I kept in contact with the Allepians—*Halabiyeh*, after we left Japan. We four siblings studied in the U.S. Frieda, Tony and I made our lives in America. Upon graduating from college, Jack went to work in Panama and Nicaragua, finally settling in Mexico.

I don't mean to exaggerate my credentials. I was lucky enough to belong to a warm and welcoming family long established in a popular destination for so many of our people. This work is mainly a series of vignettes of my family members and the wonderful individuals we had the good fortune to host, to learn from, and to enjoy.

OUR ROOTS

Ours is an oral tradition and this is what we say about ourselves: Prompted by the Spanish Inquisition, our people left Spain around the turn of the 16th century, including others from Portugal. We made our way to Aleppo where families from Italy joined our community and where we basically remained through the nineteenth century, up to the first half of the twentieth century. The effects of trade being rerouted as a result of the Suez Canal, a military draft instituted after the collapse of the Ottoman Empire, and worldwide economic downturns in the early 1900s and the 1930s spurred exoduses; the establishment of the State of Israel finalized our departure. We believe we were fifty thousand in Aleppo at our peak. Today there are no Jews in Aleppo. Our forebears formed a tightly knit society living within the same small area for some four and a half centuries. Our language was, for the most part, Arabic with a few lingering Spanish words and an abundance of Hebrew terms; and after the First World War, French.

The high level of cultural and intellectual status we attained in Spain gradually languished because of our far more restricted options under the Ottoman Turks. We could only practice professions within our own group which made doctors rare and lawyers even more so. We ceased having renowned philosophers and prominent poets, historians and advisors to those in power. Religious studies and knowledge were highly regarded. We were worldly but also orthodox. Every man aspired to pursue a career in business. After all, Aleppo was a major caravan stop and populations in the area sought work related to trade. Needless to say, the prophet Muhammad himself was a trader, permanently granting trade the prestige we took for granted. And, most importantly, our men were allowed to do anything related to promoting this important source of revenue and prosperity. Centuries of buying and selling, and bargaining for the best prices, developed and honed our superior negotiating skills. We say about anything or person of value: *sher'yeh*—a good buy. Women put their efforts into improving our cuisine, which they did to great effect. After WWI when Syria became a French protectorate, many of the children went to the *Alliance Française* where they embraced the French language, the literature, French mannerisms; and acquired a lasting heightened sense of fashion and art.

Every society tends to focus on its strengths when comparing itself to other groups. We continually stress our superior health, asserting we are made of the right *ajineh*—dough; of high quality *uhmasheh*—material; that our "Aleppo roots" are hard to rival. Thanks to the mineral content of the water in Aleppo, we generally have excellent teeth. The outstanding climate, fertile soil, the absence of chemical fertilizers and pesticides produced fruits, vegetables, grains, and meats of legendary flavor that our remarkable cooks prepared to perfection. After many years, much of the advantages of Aleppo have come to take on mythical proportions. But the foundation for such a myth must certainly have been a city with qualities conducive to exaggeration. There is not an instance in our collective memory when, in the company of family members or friends from Aleppo that *Halab*, the name of this hallowed land, had not been invoked at least once as a paradigm of something sweeter, better, finer.

From my observations, we like our food well cooked, well done, and whenever possible, served hot. That even goes for chocolate cake! And almost all of us have a sweet tooth. There are books put together by excellent chefs on our healthy, diverse, complex and delicious food, which also relate to the seasonal, the celebratory and religiously defined variations and rhythm of our menus. We owe these women our gratitude for preserving a most significant aspect of our particular civilization: Poopa Dweck's gorgeous "Aromas of Aleppo"; "Deal Delights," by the Sisterhood of Deal Synagogue; books from the prolific output of the talented Sarina Roffe, a tireless conserver of our Sephardic heritage; the original "Kosher Syrian Cooking," by Grace Sasson (not to be mistaken for Grace Sassoon). Renee Hazan, our great expert, was a phone call away, always willing to share a recipe and give guidance. Her recent demise is a huge loss for our community. She was one of the last of our pillars to fall and will be long remembered by us all. *Allah ir'hama*—May G-d have mercy on her.

For my part, I hope my accounts of my family and the unforgettable Aleppians we have known will do them justice.

A NOTE ON STYLE

I have tried different forms to demonstrate the highly prized qualities of wit and lightness that are the hallmark of our Allepians. As is true of all ethnic groups, our people talk in shorthand. We speak to each other without explanatory narrative, descriptions and embellishments which we would find tedious but might indulge in for nonmembers of the group. "Get to the point"; "hurry up" —*staj-lou*; "don't repeat"—*lat idou*; are admonishments that are either stated or hang in the air, obvious to us as we notice the annoyed look of our listeners. A big insult is to say about someone that he or she is heavy blooded. Praise is for the light blooded. The unbearable *dem il t'eel* versus the very welcome *dem il khafíf.* After trying my hand at various writing styles, I discovered that free verse captures our voices in conversation and also our impatient temperaments.

When my siblings and I left Japan our mother, to keep us in the loop, instituted the tradition of a typed weekly letter from her to all of us. In return we were expected to answer with equally detailed accounts of our activities. It is my profound regret that I haven't kept any of hers. Aside from a few narratives, I've stuck to the tempo and cadences of the way we express ourselves in order to memorialize those Syrians who left a lasting impression on me.

Names: I have spelled last names the way the individuals chose to spell them. For instance, our parents wrote Choueke with two accents, while we their children omitted these accents.

PART ONE

My Family

ONE

Brief Background

This is what I have been told: our ancestors on both sides lived in Spain for a long, unspecified time before landing in the early 16th Century in Ottoman Syria, in Aleppo. Our parents' families were living in the Jemiliyeh district of Aleppo when they left for Japan in the 1930s. First our father, Ezra Chouéké, to seek out the exporters for his boss' textile imports from there. Then our mother, Lucie Esses Chouéké, when Ezra returned to Syria in late 1936, married her as she turned 17, and took her and his mother, Farida, back to Kobe. Our father was twice as old as our mother and our grandmother 43 years her senior.

While in Aleppo, Lucie attended the *Alliance Française* school, then worked for a year at a French military office. She loved every aspect of her job: dressing up and going to work, filing, excelling in typing, bringing home a salary. Ezra's studies had been in Arabic. He spoke passable French and better English. Lucie's Arabic was fluent but French was her best language, followed by English, the lingua franca of the foreign community in Japan.

Our illiterate grandmother Farida had a reputation for her keen mind and her vast store of Arabic tales, sayings and proverbs, as well as for her outstanding talent for cooking. My three siblings and I were born in Japan, starting with our sister Frieda in 1938 and ending with our brother Tony on Armistice Day, 1945. I am the only one who visited Syria, which I did in 2006.

Farida died in 1957, at 80. And Ezra in 1991, at 88. Lucie at 100 in 2019. The three are buried next to each other in a squared lot in the Jewish section of the international cemetery high up on Mount Futatabi in Kobe, Japan. Ezra in the middle with his mother on his right and his wife on his left.

Lucie was named after her grandmother, Polissa Esses. Farida was born a Chouéké and married an unrelated Chouéké. Her husband Yaoub had a first wife from whom he had a son, Haron, for Yaoub's father. Thus, when Farida gave birth to their only child—Yaoub's second son—she could call him by *her* father's name, Ezra. But Farida had a brother called Ezra (Chouéké) who must have been called after a grandfather who by chance had the same name as his father. This is how I explain the conundrum of my father and his maternal uncle having the same first and last names.

Our brother Jack is named after Yaoub Chouéké and Tony after Simontob Esses. Our sister Frieda after Farida; while my Simone served two purposes: a substitute for Simontob in case Lucie did not have a second son; or after her mother, Setto. It also happened that Simone Simone was a popular actress at the time. The tradition persists with Jack's first son called Ezra Jack Choueke and Tony's Ezra Tony Choueke. And Jack and Tony have grandsons named after them.

When friends respectfully addressed each other, Farida was *Um Ezra*—mother of Ezra; Lucie, *Um Yaoub*, after her first born son; Ezra, *Abou Yaoub*—father of Yaoub, or Jack as he was called. There is never an *Um* or an *Abou* for daughters. In Aleppo a bon vivant was known as *Abou Lias*—father of Elias—even before he married Lucie's sister and had children. Prestige, security and responsibility fell to easily traceable sons. Daughters, unheralded, were generally considered a burden. Physically, our family was evenly divided with blue eyes for our father and two brothers, and green for our mother, sister and me. Both grandmothers had blue eyes; our grandfathers', unknown, were probably either green or blue.

TWO

Farida Chouéké

We called Farida, our
Paternal grandmother, Teta.
At sixty she left Aleppo with
The newly married Ezra and Lucie.

Thinking to spend a few months in Japan,
Twenty years later she died in Kobe.
Never reconciled to this new land, missed
Her language, weather, family, friends.

Twenty six when she had Ezra,
Considered old to be a mother
Her husband died soon after.
She doted on her cherished son.

In her room she had a free
Standing closet—*ta'a*, which
She opened infrequently and
Where she kept her treasures.

Pictures of her sister Jemoul, her
Brother Ezra, his wife Sarah and their
Children. She was sorry her Ezra
Didn't marry dignified Emilie, pretty Odette.

The closet had a musty smell.
It put us grandchildren off.
Plus, we cared little for history.
Our poor Teta, cut off from her origins,

Bound to clash, she and Lucie.
They divided their responsibilities:
Teta took over the kitchen,
Lucie joined Ezra at the office.

The ingredients for Teta's Syrian food
In the land of the rising sun:
Kamayeh—truffles, from Morocco
Batarekh—fish roe, from China,

Spices from all along the Silk Road,
Black, red and white pepper, allspice
Cinnamon, cumin, cardamom and cloves.
Local herbs: mint, thyme, parsley, coriander.

Grape leaves from our arbor. The
Rest, courtesy of Sahadi Importing
Atlantic Avenue, Brooklyn. Thankfully
Arranged by Charlie Mamiye (*Mamiyeh*).

(Charlie's illiteracy never held him back,
Even before he could start relying
On his eight children to make sense
Of the obscure written world.)

Burghol, fine and coarse; chick
Peas; lentils, yellow and red.
Pistachios, pine nuts, almonds,
Walnuts; sesame seeds, olives, oil.

Indian date paste—*teen il hindi*.
Pomegranate syrup—*ouk*. Orange and
Rose essence—*mazahe*r; dried figs, dates,
Persimmons, apricots, raisons, currants.

Teta's culinary skills fabled in
Aleppo and Japan. No one could
Match her elongated *kibbehs*,
Her incomparable stuffed onions.

For the rich and savory three
Meals a day plus extra for guests
And holidays, she strictly followed
Tradition: *Pesah* matzah from the U.S.

And all the accoutrements.
Unfailing for *Rosh Hashanah*
A kosher-killed chicken in the
Name of each grandchild.

Thursday dairy: *Mejedera*—rice with
Lentils, yogurt, spinach pie; or *calzones* and
Macaroni; or cheese *sambousak*. Eggplants
Or squash stuffed with rice and chickpeas.

Fridays: *riz ou fassouliyeh; kibbeh hamda*—
Rice with white beans; sour (lemony) *kibbeh*.
Chicken on Saturday. Sunday lunches: fava beans
With hard boiled eggs, kebabs, or raw meat *kibbeh*.

On occasion fish, always fried. Different soups.
Sometimes *kibbeh b'garaz*—*kibbeh* with cherries.
Eggplants, squash, onions, tomatoes, peppers.
Stuffed with rice and meat, or meatless.

Grape leaves wrapped around rice and meat,
Surrounded by dried apricots. Fried *kibbeh*
Nebelsiyeh—long; *kibbeh nayyeh*—raw (meat).
And daily: appetizers, salads, vegetables galore.

Teta presided, smoking (except on Saturdays),
Cursing the Japanese cook, two maids, in Arabic.
To her dismay, the cook learned to curse back.
She called the Iraqi *Um Victor* to vent.

Lavished her attention on her namesake
Frieda, talked about returning home one
Day. Of course she could never leave Ezra.
Still, nothing could assuage her nostalgia

For Aleppo. We heard about it every night
And day. Didn't listen to or hear her woes—
Severed from her family, friends and past—
Until we aged and understood the feeling.

She often used the word *wo'bah* to
Express dismay. No one would translate
It for us. I finally learned it meant plague,
An extreme and most fearsome calamity.

Farida played cards in Aleppo and Kobe.
Unable to read numbers, she counted
The hearts, spades, clubs, and diamonds,
Identified the honors from their pictures.

The help didn't try our food.
Nor Farida and Ezra, theirs.
In her last years, Teta ate
Slightly and simply: cucumber

Celery and parsley salad with
Vinegar. Rice and yogurt,
Bread and cheese. Or a piece
Of bread dipped in milk.

Our sister Frieda, the eldest,
Named for Teta Farida
Who kept her close and tied.
They adored each other.

Teta taught her grandchild to
Smoke at twelve. Frieda left
Japan before fourteen. They
Never saw each other again.

I remember our father crying in the
Hospital over *Yamo*, his mother.
Thirty four years later, when his turn
Came, he called again for his *Yamo*.

Farida Chouéké's Uhsas (Tales) & Proverbs

I. Boasting Fathers
A group of men gathered at a café
One praised his son's reliability.
Challenged to prove it
He summoned his son,

Commissioned him to kill and cook a goat,
Offer it to the company for dinner.
The son hastened to do his bidding.
The father imagined, recounted his moves:

Now he is leading the goat, now killing, now
Roasting. After several hours and many details
The father raised his hand: "*Ajjah*"—He has come.
Sure enough the son appeared with the feast.

Another man, jealous of the first's
Achievement, vowed his son could equal
The feat. Again the call arose for proof.
He summoned his son,

Ordered him to kill, cook and offer a goat.
The son ran off to obey. After several hours
The second father announced: "He's come,"
While the son struggled to untie the animal.

II. The Distracted Bride/No one Changes
The mother-in-law was warned
When the bride moved in
Of her consuming curiosity.

To put her to the test, she stated
The family custom when making *rishta*—
Noodles, was to do so in the nude.

The open window brought sounds of shouting.
The bride placed some *rishta* on her privates
And fled to witness the commotion.

21

III. The Uninvited Guest
An acquaintance arrived at dinner time
Ah'lan ou sah'lan—Welcome. *Tfedal*—
Please (partake of the meal).

The man ate and ate and ate,
Leaving little for the family.
Talab muyeh—He asked for water.

We drink water at the end of a meal,
The relieved host declared. And we
 Half-way through, the guest's retort.

IV. Someone for Everyone
Kil dist—Every pot,
Il'lo ghata—has its cover.

V. You can't have it Both Ways
A fellow *t'hamam ou khiri*—
Bathed and defecated.
Ma rah ou la ajjah—
He didn't go and he didn't come.

THREE

Frieda Choueke Saadeh

Openly Teta's favorite, our sister
Frieda indulged her rebellious streak.
In defiance of our father's prohibition
She once rode a horse, racing it in public.

After our brother Jack's long anticipated
Birth in May 1943—Kobe still mostly
unaffected by the war—our parents
Gave a big party to celebrate the event.

In the photo commemorating the
Occasion, at two and half years old,
I am sitting on our father's knee.
But there is no sign of Frieda.

The five year old collected her friends
And led them to the Evans' house. While
Sam and Fanny reveled at ours, Frieda
Freed the birds from their towering aviary.

A shocking occurrence to everyone present,
Frieda unfairly reprimanded and scolded.
In retrospect, a precocious, misunderstood
Animal rights activist, well ahead of her time.

Not obeying, reading romance comic books
At our French Canadian convent school,
Provoking the nuns to their limit,
They had no choice but to expel her.

Our parents worried about her behavior.
Finally, still thirteen, they sent her to
The Highland Manor Boarding School in
America where Syrian girls were enrolled.

Soon after she wrote that
She wanted to marry Albert,
A man from a fine, distinguished
Family. She was far too young.

Frieda attended Boston University for a
Year then married David Saadeh at 17. Our
Father travelled to the wedding in Brooklyn.
They moved to Austin for David's studies.

Nineteen and pregnant when Teta died,
David gently broke the painful news.
He said she was inconsolable not to
See her beloved grandmother again.

In 2006 Frieda died at home in L.A.
I was unreachable; in Syria, leaving
Aleppo for Latakia on that very day.
I cannot stop grieving for her.

Frieda known to be radical,
Rebellious, defiant. In retrospect
I see her brave front masking her
Fears, her extreme innocence.

Frieda and Farida, from *Ferdeh*—unique.
And so they were. I like to imagine them
Sharing a smoke, laughing and happy.
Ezra floating by, no longer admonishing.

Ta a la hon ibni—Come here my son.
Khod cigara—Have a cigarette.
Ableh rooh srakhlo la khalak—First
Go and call your (maternal) uncle

Tan dakhen kil lit na sowa—
To smoke all together. Even
Up there it could only happen
On a day other than Shabbat.

FOUR

My Sister and I

Frieda and I spoke Arabic.
She learned from our Teta,
I from our father.

Teta called Frieda *roh sitt'ek*—
Her grandmother's soul. For our
Father I was *roh abouki*—his soul.

Teta taught Frieda to cook
As did Mme (Charlie) Mamiye.
Renee Hazan had been my mentor.

Ready listeners, eager participants,
We were steeped in our culture,
Happily sought out our people.

FIVE

Setto Esses

At sixteen I left Japan for college
Going to New York via Milano
To meet *Sit*—Lady, Setto Esses, our
Famously sophisticated grandmother.

A widow with seven children by thirty,
Setto yearned for the best life; no
Housework or tending to offspring but
Couture, outings and all night gambling.

She made me buy high heels
A size smaller than my feet
And suits too tight to fit at ease.
I demurred at the suggested face peel,

Freckles O.K. with me.
Stuffed and squeezed
We made the rounds
Introducing me to society.

Unlike our Teta, Nona Setto
Was indifferent to food. Drawn
Instead to creams, cosmetics,
Fashion. But both loved cards.

No wonder Lucie never touched
Them. Wore her shoes flat, dressed
Sportily, ate heartily, slept early.
And preferred business to partying.

Setto's Advice

1. Always cream, massage and shave with upward strokes. Skin is elastic; if stretched, it will loosen and sag.

2. Guard confidences, be discreet.

3. Life is a wedding, plenty of time to rest after it's over.

4. Wear shoes a size too small.

5. Have at least one custom made suit.

6. Go regularly to the hairdresser.

7. Be graceful and agreeable.

8. Marry up financially, keep your own substantial bank account.

9. Playing cards, socializing, enjoying the good life take precedence over food, sleep and shelter.

10. Don't discuss age. Never tell yours.

Setto and *Habbt il Seneh*

The Pimple that lasts a Year

The Aleppo Evil, Aleppo Boil, One-Year-Sore.

Scientifically: the cutaneous leishmaniasis (CL)
From sandflies, mosquitos, undetermined insects,
Causing carved scars on exposed skin.

Setto had her maid draw water from a
Faraway well known not to be contaminated,
Saving her daughters disfigurement.

Setto in Aleppo

Such a pretty, fresh and stylish widow
Living a few steps from *Ahwut Ezra Chika*,
Setto went there often—*tat shouf*, to see,
Ou tin shaf—and be seen.

She often ordered a *nargileh*—
Water pipe, gossiped with friends
Loved being out among people
Refused to be stuck at home.

This despite the custom for women
To never venture in public unescorted.
Like her peers, she hired a *delal*—male
Agent, to do her errands, shop at the *souk*.

Setto and Farida's Match

As much as Farida cooked and fussed
And devoted herself to her only child,
Setto, on the contrary, fled her house

To play games, converse and mingle.
She was very attractive, likeable
And notable for her diplomacy.

Over cards Setto and Farida agreed
To match preteen Lucie Esses with
Mature, responsible Ezra Chouéké.

Before Ezra departed for Japan, Setto
Rented an *arabiyeh*—horse drawn carriage.
Lucie objected to joining them, cried.

Setto bribed her twelve year old with
Candy. On the ride she made Ezra
Promise to return and marry Lucie.

Three years later, Setto had Lucie
Photographed *à la Française*
Leaning dreamily on folded arms.

When Ezra failed to respond
Setto took a drastic step
Telegramming: *Maurice Shayo la veut.*

(Teleba—He asked for her.)
The threat quickly roused Ezra,
Brought him back to Aleppo.

Ezra, Lucie and Farida sailed to Japan
On an Italian ship in late 1936
Intending to stay a short while.

Setto finally visited Japan.
Lucie and Ezra working, Farida
Long gone, the children away.

No card games, few people
Who spoke her language,
A misplaced *femme de salon*.

Frustrated even by the
Hairdressers unwilling to
Meet her exacting standards:

The Marcel waves in front,
The French twist in back.
She wanted them just so

In a Japan where people over
Sixty were considered lucky to be
Alive. All way too dull…. She left.

After Milano, Setto settled in Buenos
Aires, always with her son David and
His family, where she died after a fall.

Setto's 1957 Day Trip to Lake Como

On our 1957 late summer excursion to
Lake Cuomo, Setto, so lovely and
So agreeable captivated our cousin's
Handsome Lebanese Christian client.

In his early thirties, twice my age,
He had eyes only for my grandmother.
He insisted that we ride with him and
Over Setto's mild objections, relegated

His mistress and me to the back seat,
Placing Setto next to him. He spoke to her
In Arabic: "*Sit* Setto," he solicitously inquired
"*Keefek?*"—How are you? "*Lazmek shi?*"—

Do you need anything? "*Ish a jiblek?*"—
What can I bring you? Even at the
Villa D'Este Hotel, he never left her side.
Over 60, perfectly coiffed and turned out,

Elegant and serene, Setto delighted
In his attentions. She commented on
How chic and well-dressed his Italian
Lady was. "*Be fudlou klebon al nass*"—

They prefer their dogs to people, he
Responded. "No, no. She is well-behaved,
She is obviously a decent woman," my ever
Diplomatic grandmother defended her.

"Don't be fooled. She is empty—*faad'yeh.*"
I remember Lake Como as a pleasant blur,
The lake, the grand hotel, the gardens, the
Wicker seating where my grandmother took

Her tea with the Lebanese at her side; her soft
Voice, her smiling lips and dark blue eyes. Now
I know what the enamored gentleman saw in
Setto: his unforgettable Middle Eastern roots.

Setto so Progressive

On Smoking:
Setto believed keeping people from
Smoking would fill the *asfouriyeh*—
Aviaries (insane asylums) to the brim.

Face Lifts:
Over sixty years ago, before
The cosmetic surgery craze,
She said of a much younger

Prematurely wrinkled acquaintance:
Lazem t'shid witcha—
She must pull her face.

Becoming Literate:
In Argentina, close to her
Seventies, Setto taught herself
To read and write a bit in French.

Setto Managing:
Setto detested penny pinching,
Scraping along on limited means,
Being financially dependent.

Her bachelor son Rafoul in
Hong Kong and daughter Lucie
In Japan took up the reins,

Gave her a sizeable allowance.
Rafoul even bought her
The fine jewelry she fancied.

Setto and Age:
Setto never told her age.
Once her eldest, Abraham
Pushed her to the limit.

Siteen–Sixty, she finally confessed.
Immi, lekan ana akbar min'nek! –
Mother, then I am older than you!

Ya'Allah, hajeh ba'ah. Lat ajis ni. —
 Oh, G-d, enough already. Don't bother me.
She succeeded in maintaining her secret.

Setto's End

When she fell in Buenos Aires, broke
Her hip, lost her appetite, I called from
New York to suggest she eat *fawleh*

B'lahmeh—string beans with meat.
I could tell it hit the mark, the familiar
Aroma filling the gulf between us.

She was in her nineties and sadly
Gone soon after. She hated to cook.
I wish I could have made it for her.

SIX

Great Uncle Ezra Chouéké

Very short, stocky, solid, handsome,
His saintly wife Sarah towered over him.
Known as *Chika* because he squinted.
He had a café and other businesses.

His bluest of eyes conjured up
The most frightening looks.
As our father would say:
Running a café is a tough man's job.

No one messed with him.
And Uncle Ezra: "I saw the whole
World; every type, shape and form
Pass through my doors."

What with buying, selling and trading in
Gold, Ezra *Chika* had many Muslim contacts.
Transmitted his affection for the Arabs to young
Ezra who forever treasured his Muslim friends.

The popular *Ahwut Ezra Chika* brought together
Muslims, Jews, Christians, all drawn there by
Il (the) *Chika,* his forceful character, his
Judgement. His reputation as a man of honor.

People came for drinks, company, his
Guidance. They admired his unbending
Honesty, his compassion for those in need,
Trusted him with their assets, their secrets.

Some played backgammon. Others
Transacted business, made deals,
Used it as their meeting place
Or a drop-off point for their couriers.

Women would often stop by,
Order coffee, perhaps a *nargileh*,
Enjoy the mixed company.
Setto, one of them.

To our father's great delight,
Many years later, in their old age
Ezra and Sarah came to Kobe
To visit him and Lucie.

Their son Albert brought a fellow
Allepian from Central America to dinner.
This man never took off his dark glasses,
Spoke loudly, gesticulated wildly.

Uncle Ezra refused to engage.
He turned his face to the wall
Indicating his disapproval, then
Went upstairs without a word.

After reluctantly leaving Aleppo for Israel
Il Chika could not regain his bearings or
Recover the pleasures of his former life, the
Joy of running his café in his venerated city.

Their children grown, finally freed from
Pregnancies, the kitchen, housekeeping,
Sarah flourished in their new home, enjoying
The help and comforts her family provided.

In Kobe Sarah loved when Lucie took
Her on her pearl business rounds
And showered her with presents,
All that Sarah's heart desired.

Uncle Ezra at his Café in Aleppo

Kobe, Summer 1960:

Sitting having dinner in the garden. Our mother stepped in the house for something. Our father, told us "He could sleep like a horse, standing up."

Jack leaned all the way down and placed his palms on the ground in front of him. He lifted his head, "Like this?"

"No, standing up, a horse sleeps standing. He would lean his back against a wall and…all he needed was a few minutes."

Our father had to speak quickly; our mother didn't appreciate the story of his uncle sleeping standing, like a horse. She would stop him when she caught him trying to tell it to us. Today was his chance and we were riveted by his account.

Seven

Ezra Chouéké (1902-1991)

Advice to His Children

Home in Kobe from university, I told our father what my Japanese Catholic friend's father said to her when she left Japan: "Don't forget your family, your country, and your religion." He liked the idea and dictated this list for me to share with my sister and brothers.

1. Remember that you are a Jew.

2. Remember your father, your mother and your siblings.

3. Do not fight with any of them.

4. Keep in mind your family, what they did for you and what they are doing for you until you will be self-supporting.

5. Ask for advice and listen to the opinion of the majority.

6. Do not make hasty decisions. Reflect before you act.

7. In society, listen before you speak.

8. If you are telling a story or a joke, don't laugh. Let others laugh at your jokes.

9. Don't gamble. If you like to play games for a pastime, only play with people that you know very well.

10. Don't hold stubbornly to your ideas. There are many people who have more experience and are cleverer than you.

11. At the table, eat slowly and moderately.

12. Keep your clothes clean.

13. Take a bath every day.

14. Don't spend more than you can afford.

15. Be honest. Don't be quick to trust in others and be very careful with everyone.

16. Don't borrow more than you can afford to repay.

17. Don't lend money to a dishonest person or to anyone that you cannot be certain will return it.

18. When you choose friends, choose those with good character and who are trustworthy.

19. If anyone plays a trick on you, don't let him do it again.

20. Always hold your temper.

21. Before booking a hotel room or ordering a meal in a restaurant, be sure you know the price.

22. Better to be self-employed. You maintain your dignity and avoid monotony.

By his example, Ezra Chouéké showed us how to be friendly, fair, generous, hospitable and charitable. We learned from him to listen to people, to see and judge them as individuals.

Ezra Chouéké Beginnings

Ezra was a rarity in our community:
An only child of an adoring early widowed
Mother. He had a devoted maternal uncle
Whose kind wife and children favored him.

His father's first wife bore him one child.
Being much older, they were hardly mentioned
And this half-brother never came to Japan.
But we did get to know two of his offspring,

Crossing paths abroad with Joseph and Maurice.
I regret I missed the sight of Haron's third son,
Jacques le Beau, reputed to be too frightening
To look at. Or was our uncle Ezra teasing me?

I'll never know or have any idea of the offending
Features of this unfortunate man, said to be
Feisty yet otherwise normal. The *Le Beau* moniker,
The reason for his notoriety.

Since our Teta Farida never mentioned
Her predecessor and *her* son, I assume
There was no love lost between Yaoub
Chouéké's two wives.

And was Haron nicknamed *Rashid*—exalted?
As was Ezra's friend Haron Djemal?
Although Ezra Chouéké had no nickname,
He was universally reputed to be wise.

Psychologically well-adjusted from his
Conflict-free upbringing with no sibling
Rivalry and not even a father to distract
His mother from attending to him.

Ezra was *shab'an*—satisfied. At school he shared
Farida's exquisite lunches with classmates. As a
Child, if his mother didn't acquiesce to a request
He would literally faint. Of course she relented.

But Ezra reciprocated his mother's devotion
Forever paying Farida the utmost respect.
He did so even though the constant rivalry
Between her and his wife made it very difficult.

Ezra's circumstances, his patience, his open
Mind turned him into a good listener.
Born intelligent, with countless friends,
His experiences translated into wisdom.

People from all over sought his counsel,
Including his wife who learned to benefit
From his incomparable scrutinizing skills
As did so many friends and acquaintances.

He dismissed no one. He took his time
Analyzing problems. His solutions unfailingly
Original and on the mark. His greatest strength
Divining how individuals act and react: judgement.

Ezra made up for his lack of siblings
With his numerous pals, his peers
Who left Aleppo in the 1930s and 40s,
Many of whom were very close.

Most happened to be natural born leaders like
Him: Rahmo Shayo; Ezra Nasser; Nessim Dwek.
Moise and Haron (*Rashid*) Djemal; Yaoub Safra; others.
These were the stars, the giants of their time.

An era of men willing and able to step up and step in.
Helpful to their families and the community, they took
Responsibility, kept confidences, did favors. They were
Respectful of others and respected in turn.

Ezra went to Kobe Japan to export the textiles he had
Imported in Aleppo. He and most of the other bachelors
Gathered at the Café Brasilero in Motomachi near the
Houses and offices they rented, by the port and the old

Oriental hotel. There were various Middle Easterners
frequenting the Brasilero. Aleppians: Murad Shalam,
Albert Chammah, Haim Djemal, Zaki Djemal, Albert Harari,
Albert Elia, Rahmo Sassoon, David (Dahude) Sassoon

The Amrams, Max Hidary (*Khedary*), Charlie Mamiye, Ezra Nasser,
Basha Hazan. And others: Saban, Carmona, Amram, Mattuck,
Kelly, d'Elia, Mizrahi, Levy. There were obviously many more
Brought to this thriving port city, pursuing exports from Japan.

Later they moved their living quarters up the hill
To the houses designed by British architects
In the 19th Century, everything constructed of wood.
The days of rickshaws, kimonos, temples.

Above all, Ezra sought and enjoyed company,
Especially that of bright and amusing people.
The Shayos, Ezra Nasser and later Grace Sassoon,
The fun loving jokester, Leon Hazan.

Shy, speaking little, Ezra let others have their say.
He seldom disputed anyone's opinion, counseled
Lucie not to "argue" with their children, allow us
To talk, make decisions, find our way.

Ezra took pride in our achievements: Lucie's, my
Sister's, brothers' and mine. In another time and
Place and given the chance, he probably would
Have been a scholar. True to his name.

Ezra with His Peers

Nessim *Nibol* Dwek:
Met as adults in Japan. An "individual"
Thing, they just clicked. Nessim and Alice
Left soon after the birth of their son.
In the 60s, embraced at a restaurant in New York,

Nessim dark, Ezra fair. Both short, sturdy,
Ordered exactly the same meal. So many
Years later, still gushing with pleasure
Joking and smiling throughout the lunch.

At his Paris office they hugged; Nessim swore
B'rahmit abi—on (G-d's) mercy for my father,
"I love you more than all my brothers combined."
And the Dweks were known to love each other.

Ezra, having grown up without siblings
His half-brother not in his life,
Overwhelmed and moved to tears by
This best compliment he could receive.

After Nessim died, Alice
Mourned him and deplored
Being on her own. She labeled it
A life of Room Service.

Ezra *Il Inglizi*–the Englishman, Nasser:
Came to Japan before settling in New York.
Sisters, Ezra *Chika*'s wife and Ezra N's mother
(Both renowned for their goodness), how Ezra
Chouéké and the Nassers related *par alliance*.

The Ezras corresponded in Arabic
Exchanging affectionate, heartfelt
Sentiments expressed in courteous,
Flowery prose. I wish I had those letters.

Ana tijar—I am a trader, our father
Would proudly declare. "Merchants
Corporation of America" Ezra Nasser
Named his U.S. business.

Unaware of foreign pejoratives
Still influenced by the prestige
Unquestionably enjoyed in Arab lands,
The Prophet Muhammad's line of work.

However, their approach to
Business could not have differed
More. Ezra N believed in maximizing
His leverage by borrowing.

Ezra C could not sleep at night
If he owed a single cent to anyone
Or to the bank. Yet the two were
Equally giving to the extreme.

Years on, Ezra Nasser invited Ezra
Chouéké and me to lunch at the
Waldorf. They spoke of this and that.
Ish biswa? —How much is he worth?

Ezra C asked about an acquaintance.
Ezra N held up three fingers, each
Standing for a million. No further
Explanation was needed.

Joe Michaan:
Over the years, Ezra spoke highly
Of his friend Joe Michaan.
I don't know when they met
Or the basis for their friendship.

Once, leaving from New York to Europe
They happened to be on the same flight.
Joe said to Ezra, "The self-employed travel
Coach," as he made his way to First.

Ezra thought well of Joe and
Appreciated his graciousness.
He spoke of this incident
As an example of fine manners.

Joe and his beautiful Egyptian wife.
Entertained often and lavishly.
My father and I were invited to their
Palatial Fifth Avenue apartment

For a most elegant sit down dinner
Where he saw many friends.
Later in a private moment in their
Library, Joe presented Suzanne

With pearls he had ordered from Japan.
They were an overtly affectionate couple.
And even more unusual, Joe encouraged
Suzanne's artistic pursuits (sculpture).

Murad Shayo:
Brother of Rahmo, also Ezra's very close
Friend. At Renee and Leon's Brooklyn
House, Murad from Argentina, Ezra from
Japan brought together as a surprise.

Both leapt up and hugged vigorously,
Identical in height and in their navy
Blue suits. Deliriously, happily reunited
After so many decades apart.

Lucie helped prepare Ezra
For his trip, packing three navy
And one gray suit. Leon, delighted,
Looked on in his usual brown.

Memories of Ezra Chouéké

The illusive Letter of Credit:
"Ish saar fil LC?"—What happened
To the LC? Our father urging by
Long distance. *"Fetahnaha"*—We
Opened it, the invariable response.

The telephone is for business,
And crises, we were told. Left
Us with a lifelong repulsion for
The ever obnoxious instrument.

Cards:
Our father could, but wouldn't
Deal anyone any hand he chose.
Expert at bridge, poker, all games,
He ended playing solitaire.

Food Allergy:
Ezra was allergic to cheese.
We kept two refrigerators,
One only for cheese.

Customers:
Our father honored his
Customers by offering his sons
For their eligible daughters.

If he had his wish, if their ages
Accorded, one would have married
Leon and Renee's daughter.

Of course Ezra never mentioned
His daughters, to anyone. Way too
Forward, unacceptably presumptuous.

Prayers:
Ezra was told that in America
Some Ashkenazi synagogues
Featured opera singers as cantors.

He longed to hear them even though
He, like all our people, found our
Chanting most moving and invigorating.

Some of our chants and prayers
Were translated into Arabic
Plus the whole Passover Seder.

As children we enjoyed the Arabic,
Understanding it over the Hebrew. On
His visits to Kobe, Leon Hazan did it best.

Ezra's Roots

Every weekend before lunch
Arabic music permeated the house.
Ezra played his treasured records:

Abdel Wahab, Fareed il Atrash,
Um Kalthum, Hannan. I disliked
Them then; later became a fan.

After I left Japan, a couple from the
Middle East travelled to Kobe.
She sang, he played the drums.

Our father, utterly entranced,
Stretched their stay from
Four days to fourteen.

A party every noon and
Night. At our house or at the
Josues'. Plus a picnic or two.

Ezra so yearned to bring the
Near East to the Far, thwarted by
Geography, climate, culture, people.

Some of Ezra's Sayings

Happiness:
Your happiness is your children and
There is no happiness without suffering.
(Be grateful for them, don't complain).

New York:
There is nowhere like it.
Who doesn't love New York?
(And so he did, on his visits.)

Mid-Life Crisis:
In Tokyo an old Middle Eastern
Man developed a sudden craze
For young women and girls.

According to Ezra, you never know
From where mid-life crisis comes, to
Whom it will happen, when or why.

In-Laws:
In-laws cannot be close. It's a
Naturally adversarial relationship.
Better to remain reserved.

Stupid People:
Never get angry
At a stupid person.
He can't help it.

Don't Generalize:
See everyone as an individual.
There are good and bad ones
Among all peoples.

Ezra Chouéké Aging

In his last years
Ezra took to his bed
His mind dimming.

It pained him on my visits home
I turned down the Turkish coffee
He enjoyed every afternoon.

Our father slowly faded
Out, speaking less to
Cover his inability.

One afternoon I grasped
For "velvet" in Arabic.
Mikhmal, he managed.

I would read him stories from
Joseph Sutton's *The Magic Carpet:
Aleppians in Flatbush*, simultaneously

Translating into Arabic the accounts
Of his acquaintances gathered in this
Wonderful book.

He looked at me confused,
Knowing I didn't read his language.
But it was easy once I got in the flow.

The voices originally in Arabic
Rendered by Mr. Sutton in English
Simply waiting to come back.

Although he urged me on and
Couldn't hear enough of them, the
Process continued to bewilder him.

In the summer of 1991
Our father was in a coma
At the Kobe Kaisei Hospital.

With our mother, my daughter
Alexandra and niece Lisa, the
Filipina live-ins, Alma and Catalina,

We were with him every afternoon.
While our mother spoke to him
I massaged his tubed arm.

One day out of nowhere,
"Charlie Mamiye," I blurted out.
His big blue eyes brilliantly lit up.

Charlie, his first U.S. customer,
Flattered Ezra when he chose him.
Admitted later because Ezra married.

After prayers over the coffin in our
Synagogue, the hearse proceeded in
A direction away from the cemetery.

Following in a taxi with Alexandra
And Lisa, I became anxious. Did the
Chauffeur err? No. An intentional

Detour. He brought the car almost
To a standstill in front of our main
Gate, before the polished brass

Plaque: Ezra Chouéké. A final farewell.
How it was done in Kobe, Japan.
The saddest moment of my life.

During the first seven days we sat
In mourning, prayers were read
Morning and night by Jewish men.

To honor our father's memory,
Frieda took charge of the kitchen.
With the help of the two Filipinas,

She served up scrumptious meals,
Full breakfasts and sit down dinners
Exactly as Ezra would have wanted.

One night *the mehshi laban*—(meatless)
Stuffed (eggplants) with yogurt, caused me
To break down. This was Ezra's favorite

Meal, and mine. I couldn't eat it without
Him and left the table for my room. Lucie
Upset at me, until she knew the reason.

The dead and the living
—*Il may'teen ou*
Il ai'sheen.

Visiting our father's grave
It suddenly came to me,
Our parents' hovering spirits.

Attached to their children,
In death they don't let go.
They stay close to us.

So when I see the offspring
Of our father's friends
It's not just me so happy.

With John Shalam, Miro Silvera, Andy
Nasser. It's also Murad, David, the two
Ezras. The spirits get a bonus: each other.

Eight

Lucie Esses Chouéké 1919-2019

Officially Polissa for her grandmother,
Lucie remembered her as "a dignified
Lady." But her mother called her Lucie,

À la Française. More often,
Lucia. For her husband, Ezra,
She was always Lucia.

His very dear friend Ezra Nasser
Arabized Lucie/Lucia to *Alouze*,
So melodious and affectionate.

He and only he called her that.
Both Lucie and her Ezra so loved
Ezra N, thrilled with his *Alouze*.

Two of her granddaughters, Lucy and
Lisa. Polissa, many centuries old,
Surely from Spain, has disappeared.

Lucie's Youth in Aleppo

The fourth of Setto's seven children
The first of her three daughters, Lucie
Was pretty, energetic, smart, fearless.

Setto out and about, the children home,
The adored Armenian maid taught Lucie
To cook, sew, wash, and iron.

At the *Alliance Française*
Lucie excelled in composition
But froze up during exams.

The Robin Hood of her class she
Forced the better off girls to share
Their lunches with her and the less off.

Skinny, always hungry as a child,
Her recurring fantasy into old age:
In a room filled with chocolate,

Eating her way out of it. So sad, when
She could afford to buy chocolates,
Obliged to watch her weight.

Aleppo in the mid-1930s
Under French rule,
A fun and modern city.

The teenagers thrived—
Westernized, enlightened,
Open to the world.

Armand Picciotto spoke French,
English. He played tennis. It was
Said of him "*Armand aime les filles.*"

He and Lucie Esses danced
Away at the monthly social.
But Lucie's mother Setto

Had already hatched her plan
To marry Lucie to Ezra Chouéké,
Her card partner Farida's son.

Setto instructed her sister Latifeh
And her husband, Khalifeh to stop
Lucie and Armand in their tracks, to

Inconspicuously approach the two
Holding up a sign: *Arrêtez*—Stop, to
Separate their niece from her beau.

The young couple pretended not to
See, dancing long into the night the
Foxtrot, waltz, the Charleston.

Ezra, seventeen years her senior
Lived far away in Japan, working to
Establish himself, building a future.

Armand, close in age, not
A serious prospect for the
Sixteen year old Lucie.

With Farida's knowledge
Setto sent Ezra a photo of
Her demure green-eyed beauty

With hair curled and highlighted in
Gold. Setto's much admired fashion
Sense caused a stir, slews of copycats.

After graduating from
The *Alliance Française*
Lucie worked for a year.

Her job typing and filing at the
French military office exhilarated
Her beyond her dreams.

She woke at dawn, put herself
To best advantage. Clean,
Well coifed, nicely dressed, she

Rode the tramcar to the office.
Her salary went straight to Setto
Except for a bit of money

She'wo'it frata—some change.
Just enough for a daily treat.
Lucie didn't mind, so happy

To be employed. Her first taste
Of paid work, the seed of her
Enduring passion.

Lucie in Japan

When Lucie married, left
For Kobe with her husband
And her mother-in-law

She knew she had to escape
The house and the kitchen,
The ever present Farida's domain.

Also, she had no interest in
Purposeless mingling; women's affairs:
Homemaking, dressing, gossiping.

She persuaded Ezra to let her
Help him in his office
Dusting the desks, filing.

Before long she was typing
His letters, meeting with
Suppliers and buyers.

After the war, she learned to
Drive, got them to the villages
Where they inspected merchandise

To be shipped to their customers
In the U.S., Canada, Europe, Central
And South America.

Ezra next to her in the black Buick
His hand on the horn; she, sitting low,
Navigating the damaged, potholed roads,

Barely missing the bicycle riders. She
Once crashed into a tramcar, blamed
The engineer for not stopping for her!

Lucie wanted to play
With the big guys
In the game of business.

But in our society
Men went out to work
To earn a living while

Women stayed home cooking,
Doing needlework, socializing,
Bringing up the children.

Almost every one of her peers
Did and enjoyed just that.
But not Lucie.

And so it gradually went
Until she earned her stripes
And moved up to tycooness.

Our men loved that
She understood the true
Extent of their success.

Not just that they provided
Fine food, luxurious shelters,
Pricey gems; but the value of

Their real estate, in her view
The very best investment
That should be held forever.

Eventually Lucie branched out,
Left Ezra to his declining exports,
Started her own pearl business.

When women looked at Lucie
They saw pearls, the ones their
Husbands would buy for them.

Men saw in her beautiful gaze
An appreciation of their net
Worth reflected back at them.

No wonder she pleased both spouses.
She gave them what they desired,
Expertly fulfilling their particular cravings.

Lucie's Mixed Signals

Lucie sought to further her education
She started reading the English dictionary
And got halfway through the A's....

In middle age, she tried to teach herself
Japanese writing. Too hard. Sorry that
She hadn't started sooner.

Lucie always read before sleeping,
Whatever came her way. Her favorites,
Bios of General MacArthur, Princess Diana.

Listening to me play (badly) the piano
She developed a taste for serious music but
Not Ezra's for opera, the voice as instrument.

Left the radio on the classical station,
With her assistant in her pearl business
Attended concerts when she could.

On the veranda by sunrise
She practiced yoga every day
Stood on her head; meditated.

I earned my bachelor's at 20
Eager to work in Wall Street but
Our mother insisted I stay in school.

When I telegrammed my news to Japan:
My Columbia master's earned with honors,
Ezra cried with joy, Lucie filled with horror.

She came to New York, to take me to Panama
And points south. Fretted and worried
About my ever diminishing marital prospects.

Who told you to get another diploma?
When you are out with an eligible man
Keep quiet, always smile and just agree.

(Sound advice, I realized in retrospect.)
We struck a bargain, I would give her a year
Then I could head to Wall Street, which I did.

Lucie Abroad

Decades after Aleppo, Lucie saw
Armand in Manila, stopping on her
Way to visit her mother in Milano.

She recounted how she finally met
Armand's wife Julia. Born an Ancona
On one side, a Silvera on the other,

Julia married a Picciotto. According
To Lucie, you couldn't get finer than
That! The aristocratic Picciottos,

Anconas, Silveras, our nobility if we
Had such distinctions. Lucie believed
These families—better educated,

Dignified, proper—set the standard for
The ideal we strived to emulate. She
Told Armand she approved his choice.

Speaking by phone from time to time,
Lucie exhorted Julia to take care of her
Boyfriend, Julia vowing she would.

Much later Lucie in New York,
Disappointed my career in Wall
Street thrilling me. The Picciottos,

Having left the Philippines, established
In Great Neck with their three children,
Invited us to dinner with Grace Sassoon

On a trip from Tokyo. Observing my
Mother with Armand, a revelation. So
Well together, tranquil, content.

Armand, even tempered, good natured
Didn't animate or disturb Lucie. The
Perfect antidote to her exuberance.

Armand reached her core, gave her
Peace. Julia now also part of their
Ever pure and innocent bond.

Lucie's first trip to N.Y. setting
Frieda up at the New Jersey
Highland Manor Boarding School.

In Bradley Beach watching
A backgammon game,
The stakes were high.

Lucie imagined the aqua Buick
She bought to sell in Japan,
The profit to cover her trip,

Moving swiftly from one
Player to the other, their
Poker faces disclosing nothing.

She, the only woman aware of
The value of the bets. A business-
Woman among her male peers.

Lucie a noticeable exception
Where Sephardics and Ashkenaze
Were more like strangers.

As much as our people
Kept away from the Ashkenaze
Lucie was drawn to them.

She liked the customers
She and Ezra exported to
In Canada, Panama, Venezuela.

She laughed heartily at their jokes.
*My Yiddisha Mamma, Fiddler on the
Roof* her favorite song and show.

On stays in New York and Montreal
She gravitated to the delis,
Ordering salami or pastrami on rye.

She drew the line on gefilte fish,
Something only her friend Grace
Actually tasted and liked.

Lucie took me along to Washington
To retrieve our deposits at U.S. banks
Seized by the Government during WWII.

Too costly to bother, the lawyer counselled.
Nothing personal, just collateral damage,
He explained. She understood, accepted.

The elevator at our Jefferson Hotel
Stopped, V.P. Richard Nixon entered.
Smiling broadly, he shook Lucie's hand.

"If I was American, I would vote for you,"
She told the baffled presidential candidate.
We met her old bachelor distant cousin.

He invited us to an Arabic restaurant.
Can I say I've been to Washington?
Yes, sort of. Lucie's Washington…

My mother arranged for us to
Meet at the Grand Hotel in Paris,
She from New York, I from Brazil.

An October midnight
And as usual with Lucie
She had not reserved ahead.

The Lebanese manager insisted
No room was to be had.
Persuaded or worn down

He gave us the bridal suite
For the price of a double.
Everything in satin and velvet

An enormous heart shaped tub
A 360 degree view of the city.
Lucie never one to spend

On fleeting amenities, so
When Dr. Joseph Dwek arrived
To take us to dinner she

Insisted he come up for a
Drink. She reveling, I mortified
In all that doggone pink!

Lucie had sent some figurines
To the relative of an acquaintance
For his shop in Paris.

He received them but never paid,
Giving excuse after excuse, finally
Not even answering her letters.

The next evening Lucie and I went
Unannounced to his apartment,
Knocked on the door which he

Opened slightly. Lucie pushed her
Way in, recognized her statues
Displayed on his mantelpiece.

She headed straight for them,
Took the coral, handed me two
Jades. And we walked right out.

He blabbered some explanation
Pointedly ignored by Lucie
Who never looked back at him.

Unafraid, just as years before
With the Japanese *dorobo*—thief,
Now confronting this Egyptian *voleur*.

There was something about offices
That Lucie could not resist.
Reminders of her job in Aleppo?

So we visited customers, friends
And acquaintances the world over
At their place of business:

In New York and Montreal
Panama, Milano, Manila,
Taiwan and Hong Kong.

Lucie spent hours rustling up orders,
Ironing out the minutest details of
Fees, tariffs, costs, shipping dates.

An irresistible phenomenon,
Attractive, fascinating, one of their
Own. And knowledgeable to boot.

Needless to say I found it annoying.
But seeing how much it pleased
Her, how could I deny her this fun?

I followed obediently, sat quietly,
Waiting for the ordeal to end,
The clothes shopping to come.

A cousin in Milano recommended
We go to vacation locales where our
Young people met and matched up.

Lucie disregarded the well-meaning
Lady's misguided notion. After all,
Didn't all our men go to their offices?

The Fur Coat

Story told to me by Rachel Safdie (*Safdieh*), Corroborated by Lucie

Lucie Chouéké, on a trip from Japan, called Rachel Safdie when she landed in New York, requesting her help in finding a fur coat on her forthcoming trip to Montreal.

Rachel lined up three appointments, starting with the least expensive shop and ending with the one with the highest quality wares. Sure enough, at the third stop a $6,000 mink coat caught Lucie's eye. She tried it on; she had Rachel and a female employee of the establishment try it on. She directed the salesman to ask his manager for a reduction in the price. The man returned with a $5,000 offer. Lucie put on the coat again, had Rachel model it and opine further on its merits. Then she opened her handbag so that the salesman could see the bills and told him she had $3,000 in cash; and if the manager agreed, she would part with it all and take the fur back to Japan. Rachel, very properly brought up in England, thought she would go through the floor.

The salesman returned and announced that they had a deal. Not satisfied with her coup, Lucie negotiated for a belt to match and extra pelts to be made into a hat. She was given everything she requested.

When Rachel returned home, she reported to her husband Leon on what had happened. Leon responded with a single word: "Learn."

P.S. On her way back to Japan, Lucie made a stop in Mexico where she found the coat a receptive owner and a suitable closet in which to hang.

Lucie Chouéké's Maxims, Sayings & Advice

Charity begins at home.

Ba'ed ou sa'ed—Send far and help. (Don't hold onto your children.)

Put down roots where you land.

Make good friends.

For every five times you invite someone, you are lucky to be invited back once.

Jewelry is a waste.

Wearing fur, the skin of a poor animal, is barbaric.

Have a comfortable and well-designed home.

Dress simply. Keep your nails short and natural.

Use yogurt or cucumber and egg whites for a facial mask.

Stay active to be healthy of mind and body.

Read for knowledge and pleasure.

Travel.

Food is the most difficult part of travel.

Marriage: once is enough.

Marry to have children when you are young. Then concentrate on working.

There's nothing equal to the pleasure of work. Each day brings something new and interesting. You can be creative and forget problems and minor cares.

Invest your profits in real estate.

Every business trip is profitable.

To make money, you have to spend money.

Sleep is #1; food #2; exercise #3; and work, work, work.

There is no shame in any work. Indolence is shameful.

Chacun son métier et les vaches seront bien gardées.

Farmers are the best people: hardworking, down to Earth, unpretentious.

A gentleman or a lady, is a well behaved person.

P.S. Lucie enthusiastically proclaimed: "Ezra Nasser is a gentleman, a farmer." Her ideal man.

Nine

Lucie and Ezra Chouéké

Not a marriage
That would have taken
Place if not arranged.

A big difference in their ages
Temperaments, interests, energy.
The way they looked upon life.

But they had in common
Their love for their children
Their kindness to anyone in need.

Overall, it worked well.
Ezra gave Lucie free reign
To develop her potential.

Lucie admired Ezra's intelligence
Sought and followed his advice
Respected his decisions.

Ezra felt best amongst our people
Their shared language, humor,
Affection for each other, hospitality.

In Ezra's over 55 married years in Japan
Only Syrian food was ever served
In their house, and offered to all.

After our Teta died, Ezra took over
Planning the menus. His refined,
Discerning palate regularly spot on.

Our Japanese cook expertly produced
The Syrian specialties she and the maids
Avoided in favor of their own food.

Ezra wanted to cook, inventing
Dishes that somehow never quite
Met his expectations.

On the few occasions when Ezra
Put his hand to preparing a meal,
Lucie forewarned the children

Not to complain or to make any
Negative comments, but to only
Praise the results of his efforts.

Ezra, no fool, grasped Lucie's
Intervention. But also the primacy
Of her discriminating, proper behavior.

Lucie ate literally everything.
She was open to all peoples, ideas,
Nationalities, social and economic levels.

She loved land, Ezra, stocks.
At the office, Lucie itching to get to
Work; Ezra's priority, organizing lunch.

Ezra wise, therefore cautious,
Proud of his very dynamic wife,
So street smart, tough and gutsy.

We once had a burglar—*harami.*
Ezra pulled the covers up tight.
Lucie leaped out of bed shouting

And throwing her slipper at the
Startled Japanese *dorobo* who
Ran for his life, never returned.

We were awed by her bravery.
With age, brave appears foolhardy,
Ezra's inaction much more sensible.

A woman came to Japan
Part of her worldwide travels
Raising funds for needy children.

Her stories told at our synagogue
Moved everyone to tears.
Except for Ezra…

He maintained her accounts were
False, that she was a sham, that
No funds would reach any victims.

The community took issue with Ezra,
Accused him of being hardhearted. Lucie
Believed the woman, but said nothing.

A few months later, press notices reached
Kobe. The woman a blatant thief, her
Fake cause an international fraud.

Lucie spoke to us: "Your father is very
Intelligent. He understands people.
He is the best judge of character."

Above all respect reigned between
Them. Their relationship
Never less than dignified.

They only travelled separately,
Because of the children, business.
Ezra's conduct never changed.

Anywhere and with everyone
He maintained his dignity.
Modest, moderate, a gentleman.

Lucie on her own let loose:
Arabic dancing on tabletops,
Singing in French, joking,

Talking a blue streak,
Laughing too loudly. So
Very unlike her husband.

Her drive, her suppressed
Vitality, bursting forth with
Overwhelming earthy delight.

She restrained herself around
Ezra, knowing he wouldn't
Care for such overt displays.

Ezra cried easily, Lucie very
Seldom shed a tear. Yet they
Made each other whole.

Lucie at her best under Ezra's
Firm hand and guidance. Ezra
Secure through Lucie's efforts.

Both most enjoyed New York,
On and around Fifth Avenue,
The streets in the 30s and 20s.

Their importer and wholesaler
Customers, friends, acquaintances.
Mamiye, Hidary, Shaya Shalom

Sutton, Azrak-Hamway (*Hamoui*),
Mishan, Hazan, and more. Nicely,
Conveniently clustered as in the souk.

They walked down Fifth from "Ezra
Nasser's" Empire State building to the
Broadway intersection at 23rd Street.

Meeting, bumping into friends, popping
Into their stores, warehouses, offices. Prime
New York real estate transformed into *Halab*.

Ezra lunched at the Arabic restaurants
Listening to, laughing with his Aleppo pals.
Lucie at the Automat or a coffee shop.

Ezra was driven by Charlie Mamiye's sons or
Leon Hazan in their cars, Lucie took the subway.
Following Charlie's instructions, she always asked

Three different people for directions. Exasperating
Getting their attention, finding answers on a
Crowded platform as we ran to catch a train!

She focused on generating orders,
Collecting past due payments. Female,
Striking, unique, a force of nature.

She had no patience for small talk.
"Constructive" her favorite word.
Ezra, the Syrians, got a kick out of her.

The difference between Ezra and Lucie:
He an only child; she, one of seven.
Lucie could rough it, Ezra could not.

Ezra's high morals clashed
At times with Lucie's
Practical and realistic bent.

In the mid-1970s Ezra was
Offered multiples of what he paid
For the small office building in Osaka

Purchased from Moche Nessim when
The Nessims immigrated to Brazil.
Paid the equivalent of $20,000 for it.

The price Ezra accepted, converted
To dollars, some 20 times this sum.
He gave Lucie the good news.

She insisted he turn it down.
But he had given his word!
She refused to budge.

Ezra, humiliated, held his ground.
Lucie, outraged he would consider
Selling without her consent.

Finally, Ezra very apologetically
Told the agent how sorry he was to
Retract, only to be given a higher price.

Lucie turned it down and the others
That followed until they reached
Two and a half times the original offer.

Ezra saw himself as a man of honor
Who reneged on his word to the
Person who brought him the proposal.

Lucie perceived this fellow as a cover for
A faceless corporation with bottomless
Funds. Her accurate reading sealed the deal.

Not that Ezra was ever reconciled.
He could not accept he betrayed his
Principles, going back on his promise.

Ezra represented the old, dying traditions.
Lucie fully embraced modern practices,
What so perplexed and dismayed Ezra.

Regardless of Lucie's strength and realism,
She eagerly sought Ezra's counsel,
Deferred to his excellent judgement.

Frieda at 14, wrote from America
Stating she wished to marry, a fellow
Syrian from a fine family.

Lucie, frantic, discussed it with her best
Friend Lucie Nessim, whom she idolized.
They agreed an immediate response

Was in order, explicitly commanding
Frieda to abandon this outrageous
Idea. Ignoring their badgering,

Ezra took his time, telling Lucie
He would think about it.
Finally, after a few days

He gave his reply: Unfortunately,
Her parents were far away and
Could not meet the young man.

Frieda would have to take responsibility
For her decision. They trusted her.
Frieda wrote back that she would wait.

Ezra, well adjusted, consistently ethical,
calm, reflective, fair. He solved problems,
Headed off conflicts. A perfect judge.

Lucie, cool, at times impetuous, interested
In building her business, forging ahead.
With Ezra's support, she reached her apogee.

Ten

Lucie Chouéké's Greatest Triumph

In her sixties, Lucie went through a pivotal time. Soon after moving out of the office building he sold, Ezra was diagnosed with prostate cancer and his overall health declined. Eventually, in his 80s—in the 1980s—he closed his business and stayed at home. With the booming Japanese economy and the heightened value of the yen, Japan became very expensive for tourists from abroad. Also, pearl prices rose and Lucie's orders shrank. Ezra actually enjoyed retirement: no more commuting to Osaka; hanging out instead at the Kobe Club where he saw friends and acquaintances; going to the Daimaru Department store or even to an occasional movie with Dahude Sassoon's brother, Yaoub, on long visits from Turkey. Lucie found such activities excruciatingly boring: small talk, idle days, not being constructive, not having a purpose were her nemeses. What Ezra took pleasure in, she deemed punishment.

A Japanese scroll hanging in their bedroom depicted carp floating underwater. Lucie took to gazing at it for hours. She reminded herself of the Japanese saying that carp have to hit bottom before they can rise to the surface. She saw herself falling but her perennial optimism held on to the thought of a renaissance for her—a new direction, a business that would keep her busy, prove profitable and that she could do from home where Ezra increasingly took to his bed. In the meantime Kobe was becoming an attraction for multitudes of Japanese who wanted to see the "romantic" and "exotic" city where foreigners had lived and their distinct houses which were being opened to the public for a small fee. Choueke-te (Choueke mansion) had been designated a national treasure. It was the house that the talented British architect, Alexander Hansell designed and built for himself in the late nineteenth century—the most beautiful of all the houses he completed in Kobe and one that survived intact the carpet bombing of the city in 1945.

A note about our experience during the war in Japan. Since we were considered Syrian nationals and therefore neutral, the officials treated us exactly as they did the native population and subjected us to the same rules, restrictions, and food rationing. The Americans gave prior warnings of planned bombings, especially of urban centers. This is why, in early 1945, the chief of police instructed all residents of Kobe to evacuate before the expected disaster. Our family, together with other Middle Eastern and some European foreigners, spent most of the last year of the war in the countryside, huddled in mud cottages before returning after the Armistice to an almost totally destroyed Kobe. Our big Victorian style house (also designed by Alexander Hansell) and all the furnishings had burned to the ground. Luckily, our father found a nondescript two story edifice across the street from where it had stood and purchased it for some sixty bolts of satin fabric he had in inventory. Less than nine years later, in 1954, our parents bought Alexander Hansell's own house.

The first thing our Teta did after our parents signed on Hansell's house was to cut down the fig tree growing in the garden. According to her superstitions, fig trees caused people to move from their homes. She didn't need to consult with her son and daughter-in-law. No one would defy Farida's judgement and any decision she made in such matters. And so it happened that she and our parents stayed in the house until the end of their lives.

Kobe City Hall

Kobe, Japan

July 23, 1960

Mr. Ezra Choueke

No. 40, Yamamoto-dori, 3-chome

Ikuta-ku, Kobe

Dear Mr. Choueke:

Your house was designed and built in September 29, 1896 by the late
A. N. Hansell, an Englishman. He lived in Kobe at that time and worked as one
of the best architects here. He built many excellent buildings. Among his works
were the then Kobe Foreigners Club house and Hongkong Shanghai Bank building. Unfortunately, however, these buildings were lost in the war.

I am now studying the history of Japanese modern buildings. I have
found out that your residence was built by the late Hansell as his home after con-
tacting his daughter who lives in Monaco now. On my investigation of the old
wooden buildings which now exist in Kitano-cho or Yamamoto-dori areas, I have
found out that your house is the best one there.

Your house fortunately escaped from war damage and we are proud of
having such an excellent building as yours. Therefore, it is our earnest desire that
you will take good care in maintaining your house, taking its significance into our
consideration.

Yours sincerely,

K. Sakamoto

Katsuhiko Sakamoto

Member

Modern Buildings Survey Committee
Japan Architecture Association (Incorporated Association)

In the 1980s, the increasingly flush Japanese travelled to Kobe from all over the country, passing by our house enroute to the *ijin-kans* (foreigners' Western style residences of the Meiji period) they were scheduled to visit. Being told by their guide that it was occupied, they occasionally threw small stones at the windows to catch the attention and a glimpse of our family members. City officials approached our parents to ask if they would open the house as an *ijin-kan*. But how could it be done while Lucie and Ezra lived in it? Under no circumstances would they leave the house. And so Lucie came up with the idea that she could open just the downstairs and the garden; not the upstairs and the separate kitchen with the maids' quarters above it.

She asked Ezra and, although we all lived far away, each of her children separately for an opinion. Ezra told her to do as she wished. Frieda objected. She wanted on her stays to be able to come down to the kitchen in her *yukata* (light kimono) and to have the use of the living and dining rooms. Our brothers were indifferent. I was enthusiastically for it. It would be the only owner-occupied "museum," as it was called. And Lucie would run it without interference from the government. The Mayor was delighted as this, the grandest of all the *ijin-kans*, with old time residents still in place, would be a fantastic added attraction and another boost to Kobe's now thriving new source of income. She opened it in October 1986 and it proved to be an immediate and huge success. The Mayor turned out to be right.

Not until her late sixties did
Lucie strike gold, her house
Transformed into a museum.

The Japanese rushed in,
A veritable flood, buying
Everything on display: the

Homemade *ma'moul* cookies,
Scarves, Mexican T-shirts, soap,
Watches, children's clothes.

Lucie cleared out all Ezra's
Old samples gathering dust,
From pens to underwear.

We laughingly begged her
To be very careful
Not to sell our father!

By that time he had taken
Full-time to his bed, occasionally
Surveying the action on a monitor.

At dawn Lucie already up. After
Exercising, showering, and a quick
Breakfast, ready to seize the day.

Not to waste time, Lucie stuck
To her uniforms. In summer, white
Embroidered Mexican T-shirts,

White slacks. In winter, Montreal
Eaton's white cotton turtlenecks,
Black slacks, fur vests from Frieda.

Lines formed before eight:
Simple folk from villages,
T.V. and movie celebrities,

Housewives and school chums
Traveling on reunions,
Prince Mikasa from Tokyo.

Peasant and nobility all treated the
The same. Children and the disabled
Admitted without charge.

Choueke-te the only place
Where farmers and aristocrats
Rubbed shoulders, hosted by Lucie.

They had free reign of the
Downstairs and the garden.
A real treat for the curious

Japanese who yearned to see
Our British designed house
And how foreigners lived

In their country, in their midst,
So far from the birthplaces
They had left behind.

Lucie's commitment to stay
Forever reassuring them Japan
Was special, as they believed.

Couples requested to be married
On the tiered well-tended lawn.
Ever positive, Lucie made it happen.

She let the brides dress upstairs
In Teta's and later my old bedroom,
And hired a minister to officiate.

Mr. Burke, keen to work,
Gladly obliged, proficiently
Administering ecumenical rites.

All this in the middle
Of guests streaming through
The house and garden.

These weddings took place
Among family, friends, Lucie,
The help and the general public.

The house did happen to be
A Victorian architectural gem.
Ezra had filled it up eclectically

With silver, ivory, coral and jade,
Woodblock prints received in
Settlement from a bankrupt supplier.

Hand embroidered tablecloths,
Chairs upholstered in petit point,
Persian and heavy Chinese carpets.

Dishes galore. Enough sets of
Noritake, Satsuma, Imari ware
To fill a few shops.

Lucie transformed the foyer
Into a veritable bazaar.
Strangers appreciatively

Observing all very well and
Good, but she had to sell
To satisfy her ambition.

Such big crowds all
Exuberantly on vacation
Ready, willing, able to spend.

She strategically placed a
Toaster oven to heat the *ma'moul*,
Seducing the guests with the aroma.

The *ma'moul* her best item,
Preferable to *ka'ik* and *sambousak*.
The Japanese love sweets.

The scarves with a former maid
Demonstrating how to tie them,
The second most sought-after item.

Third came the all-natural olive oil
Soap I imported from Greece.
A balm for the many with allergies.

To add a personal touch, I took the
Small black and white photo of Lucie
Posing *à la Française*, the one Setto

Sent to Ezra; had it blown up to the
Max. To brighten the effect, I searched
For a long stemmed red velvet rose.

Found the perfect bud in a fabric store,
Placed it along the bottom edge.
This would be what the guests

Would see immediately upon
Entering the house, prompting
Great interest in this stunning girl.

That it represented an *Omiai*
(*Bazra*, match) picture resulting
In Lucie's marriage to Ezra

Fascinated the visitors, many of
Whom went through a similar
Process before they married.

They were brought into Lucie's
Personal life: her home, her past,
Her beginnings and her present.

Not that Lucie paid much attention
To my efforts which she found
Time consuming and unnecessary!

She also thought little of the tiring
Way I sold: studying the products,
Patiently pitching them on their merits.

She preferred short-cuts.
For the soap: "I use it."
The *ma'moul*: "I made it."

The decorated Mexican T-shirts
I discovered which she wore:
"You see, they are my favorite."

No one could help but succumb to
Her charisma, to admire her power.
She had "it." I did not.

Once during the very festive
Five day Golden Weekend,
I watched as Lucie shook

Some 8,000 hands, placing
A bag of *ma'moul* in each
Until the kitchen ran out.

Scarves, soap, pearl rings,
Philippine cushion covers,
All flying out of the house.

Such revenues and gratitude
Warmed Lucie's heart. She gave
Her all to please her "guests."

Never a snob, Lucie welcomed
Everyone equally, encouraged
Them to feel at home.

They begged to be photographed
Holding her hand; and politely
Asked for her autograph.

Her undeniable magnetism
Soon discovered by the press:
Television, newspapers, magazines.

The media couldn't get enough of
Polissa-san, her captivating way of
Speaking the Kansai dialect—

The language of the common folk
In our area: direct, casual, informal,
Roughish. So different from the refined

Kanto speech of the Tokyo region,
And of the educated, the upper class.
Or those aspiring to appear refined.

She was mesmerizing, approachable,
With nonstop energy. She kindly and
Readily answered all their questions.

Of course the never ending publicity
Magnified the interest in her
And the ever popular Choueke-te.

Terribly exciting times,
Continuous stimulation
While the profits poured in.

Lucie said she would have
Been willing to pay
For all the fun she had.

Visitors sat on the sofas and chairs,
Chatting and gazing at the pictures
Of Lucie's scattered family.

Marveled at her grandfather
In his typical Syrian garb who
Lived well beyond 100.

A party every day
So much laughter
Excitement and joy.

They loved her and
She loved them back.
Elated by her newfound fame,

She basked in the limelight.
Producer, director and star
Of her own remarkable show.

In 1992, a year after Ezra died,
Lucie succumbed to a depression
From which she recovered,

Only to be confronted with the
January 1995 Kobe earthquake.
The long and stressful ordeal

Of restoring her house to
Its original state and dignity
Finally did her in.

She spent the rest of her life in
Her bedroom, apologizing. Not
Used to being dependent.

Lucie's accomplishments in her maturity
Included serous volunteer work. She
Served on Kobe's panel on tourism.

She and Ezra ever on the giving end,
Unaccustomed to asking for donations.
Lucie extended herself, solicited funds for

The Synagogue earthquake damage repairs.
Fifi and Edmond Esses heeded her call.
Their generous contribution dwarfing

All the others made her effort worthwhile.
From the outset, Lucie set aside 10% of
Her museum's daily revenues for charity.

The practice carried out with a big glass
Jar on top of the front reception desk,
Overflowing with yen by the end of each day.

Ezra did not tell her to do so but
Always in favor of service, he was
Proud of her decision to tithe herself.

We sought treatment for her in
Kobe, Tokyo, California. Finally
Advised she should stay in her home.

The museum continued to operate, the
Fall 1996 reopening presided over by
The Duke of Kent, come to cut the ribbon.

Lucie dragged herself out of bed
Valiantly present at the ceremony, but
Too fragile to resume her commitment.

British Consulate General

Osaka 24 November 1996

Mrs Polissa Choueke

Choueke House

3-5-17 Yamamoto-dori

Chuo-ku

Kobe 650

Dear Mrs Choueke,

Having just returned from seeing off His Royal Highness The Duke of Kent on his return flight to London, I wanted to write straight away to say how extremely grateful I am to you, to your daughter Simone, and indeed to your entire household for going to such enormous trouble to receive His Royal Highness so splendidly in your home last Saturday.

It was particularly good of you to do so when I know you have not been feeling well recently. I know His Royal Highness greatly appreciated that, and was most impressed by your beautiful home and all the beautiful things in it.

But above all, I would like, if I may, to pay tribute to the very major contribution you have made to the conservation of Kobe's early history through the maintenance of your splendid house. We are honoured that you allowed British specialists to play a part in its restoration, and delighted to learn that you are satisfied with the quality of their work.

Thank you once again for everything you did to make this important part of His Royal Highness's programme an outstanding success.

Yours Sincerely,

David

David Cockerham

HM Consul-General

84

Eleven

Lucie's Last Years

After the Duke left, Lucie ended
Up doing what she abhorred, what
Ezra had done against her pleas:

Spending her last 23 years in her bedroom.
Thus Lucie's retreat from active life began
At 77. For all her maxims and convictions

She missed social interactions. Wished she
Had friends nearby. Yearned for connection,
Conversation, the idle banter she had shunned.

She made do in her house with Catalina,
Her sunny, devoted Filipina housekeeper,
Visits from family members; tourists; paid visitors.

Deeply appreciated, my saintly school friend
Ana Maria Leonhardt took it upon herself to
Cheer up and be there for Lucie and Catalina.

Lucie wanted her children with her but
In Japan. They were long abroad. *Ba'ed
Ou sa'ed*. This is how it turned out.

Her complexion remained true to her
Aleppo *Crème Fraîche* pet name,
All the way to the end of her nineties.

We now had countless hours to talk
And Lucie wanted to look back,
To analyze and consider her life.

Her early years in Japan
Were the most difficult.
Her babies in wartime,

Bombings, running for shelter,
Food shortages, electricity outages,
The constant fear; losing her home.

But the rest of her 83 years in Kobe
She determined were better than
Anywhere else she could have been.

She wished she could hear
Um Kalthoum sing *Enta Amri*.
I played it on YouTube.

It moved me to tears.
I don't know if she liked it.
"It's very sentimental,"

Lucie's dry-eyed response.
The stark difference between
Her and Ezra (and me).

Lucie's Reflections in her Own Words

I missed my old friends. Far away, especially school friends. And my children being far.

I regret not knowing my father. I have only one vague memory of my father. He was in bed, looking in the distance. I was less than five years old. I asked him to buy me a bracelet and he promised me he would as soon as he could get up. He never did again. I don't even have a picture of him. Some people said he looked like my older brother, Abraham. I learned later that he did a lot of charitable deeds, especially for orphans.

Syria was a French protectorate when we were growing up. I studied French and admired French culture. But school in Aleppo was really too much about France and too little about other subjects. We had to know almost as much about Paris as a French child. What use was that? I haven't spent more than a month in France in my whole life. But French, France and the French were our ideal in language, culture, our taste in furnishings and clothes.

I was an excellent student. My number one subject was composition. I have always written many letters—to family, friends and for business. I am told that I express myself well. My children have taken after me, they also write often and well. It is also a matter of practice. We still write and we prefer writing to the telephone.

In Aleppo we lived in a real community—relatives, friends in housing complexes with shared courtyards. (Lucie's grandparents lived this way, Lucie and her parents and siblings lived in a low rise building with a balcony, most often covered and giving onto the street.) It was a concentrated population with a lot of interaction and people always aware of what others were doing, a check on each other. This led to a very organized way of living and acting, very much like in Japan.

Even in our language, like in Japanese, there are phrases and expressions for almost every occasion: a special greeting when someone returns from a trip, when finishing a meal, when speaking of the dead. Very strict rules and customs for correct behavior, like in Japan. Maybe that's why we found mutual respect here. I am sorry I didn't learn to read and write Japanese. If I could do it over again, I would start as soon as I arrived in this country. I tried after the children grew up but it was too late. The *kanji* is very difficult.

What makes Japan so special for me? The people, their courtesy and good manners. I love the nature here, the climate and the culture. My best memories are here. And I love my current life, mixing with the general population, having a purpose. I am very grateful to the Japanese for letting us live among them as equals. During the war they were as concerned about us as they were about their own people. I don't think I could have been as happy anywhere else in the world.

What are my strengths? I am healthy, optimistic. I have courage. I am flexible and tolerant of all people. I have the ability to encourage others. Of course they saw how happy I was to work so they also worked.

And my weaknesses? My impatience with small talk, with idle social life.

What is my philosophy? To work, to be self-sufficient, to treat everyone the same. To be in harmony with nature, to be charitable and to personally help others. My grandfather worked when he was over a hundred, until the last day. Why stop? With every year you gain more experience and knowledge. Retiring brings loss to a country. Work lets you maintain your dignity and keeps you healthy. My friend Nakai-san, the former mayor of Kobe, he is 102. I admire him. He is my idol.

My husband was flexible and intelligent, he was pleased and proud of my accomplishments but I think he missed my company, passing hours at the clubs, playing cards. We never traveled together.

Lucie's Final Days October 2019

Her depression of over two decades
Lifted. Her dear Catalina, my friend
Natasha and I hovered around her bed,

Natasha telling funny stories
Of her past and present in her
Beloved birthplace, Kobe.

Natasha's sister Daria
Returning to California
Came to say goodbye.

She kissed Lucie on the forehead.
"You're coming back?" Lucie, ever
The optimist, asked Dari-*chan*.

During her last days, when alone,
Lucie and I spoke mostly in Arabic.
We'll have a party to celebrate

Your 100th. She smiled radiantly.
I mentioned the heavy
Aleppo dishes served at feasts:

Sfiha—stuffed veal pocket.
Ji'at—stuffed intestines,
Thankfully seldom served.

Kamayeh—truffles
Batarekh—fish roe.
"Ha, ha," she giggled.

And after each suggestion,
"I am happy. Are you happy?"
Yes of course, I responded.

Would you like to take a trip?
"Yes."
With whom?

No answer.
Your sisters?
"Yes, yes."

She remembered her trip
Before her last depression.
Her clear green eyes

Bright and shining
Her skin glowing
"Open the curtains,"

She instructed Catalina,
"Turn on the lights."
The first time in 23 years.

I had tried to recall
Charlie Mamiye's wife's name.
Simha.... It came to me too late.

It constantly frightened Lucie
To think of herself underground.
"Above ground is better," her truth.

Twelve

The Futatabi Cemetery

High up on the mountain near
A lake, pine trees galore, songbirds
Everywhere. A few polite hikers.

I don't know of and can't imagine
A more beautiful and peaceful
Cemetery in the whole world.

Aside from the three Chouékés,
There are another three Aleppians
Whose remains rest in Kobe:

Moise Bigio, Olga Sassoon Josue
And her husband Gaby Josue.
Our people, some 20% of the total,

Buried in the Jewish section of the
Futatabi International Cemetery.
A percentage certain to decline.

Thirteen

Uncle Rafoul Esses

Rafoul and his sister Lucie
Were as close as siblings could be.
Rafoul, eccentric and different,

Far from the typical Syrian.
Exceedingly considerate, good, straight
Beyond the norm, the best of us.

They agreed they would care for
Each other as they aged. Sadly,
Lucie's depression negated her

Promise to him. And his death cut short
His to her. No homage can do him justice.
I've never known a better human being.

Rafoul, our only other family member
In Asia. For lack of any citizenship,
Trapped for decades in Hong Kong.

We all included Hong Kong in our
Travel plans, to call on Lucie's
Precious, stranded brother.

Slight of build, nearsighted,
Incredibly caring and giving,
He spent 40 years on Nathan Lane.

Every evening he made his way
To the landmark Peninsula Hotel
Meeting up with his many friends.

Took up walking, healthy living
But too late to fend off three
Cancers: throat, lung and brain.

Never realized his dream
To settle in a home. Perhaps,
Too, for a wife, for children.

He started off selling LPs,
Then became an exporter
To customers Ezra Chouéké

Forwarded to him from Japan.
Although from Aleppo where
Taf-seel—haggling, a way of life,

And landed in the Chinese culture
Where bargaining par for the course,
Uncle Rafoul refused to "negotiate."

His reasoning: he couldn't
Accept depriving his suppliers
Of making a decent living.

Dahakou ah leh—
They laughed at him.
Until quotas were set…

Permission to export based
On past shipments soared in
Value, coveted in the trade.

He could sell his every year.
T'zen gan—he got rich,
Min ghas min annoh—

In spite of himself.
Nassibo—his fate.
A well-deserved one.

Moe Hidary came to him
Via Kobe. They hit it off,
Enjoyed a lasting friendship

Spending evenings at the Peninsula,
Smoking, eating, drinking, playing
Tawleh (backgammon) and gin rummy.

Doris and Victor Shalom also
Became very close friends
He seldom lacked for company.

His family, his good friends
Appreciated this finest of
Individuals, this man from Aleppo.

Lucie Esses, Aleppo 1936

Lucie Chouéké, Fortuné Hazan, Adéle Saban, Kobe, Japan 1937

Top, Passover Kobe, Japan 1937.
Front right Lucie Chouéké, Front
left Farida Chouéké, Behind Farida
Chouéké, Ezra Chouéké

Below, Party Celebrating Jack's
Birth. May,1943, at the Chouékés'
first Alexander Hansel designed
house. It was destroyed by the
Allied bombing of Kobe in 1945.
Lucie is in front on right. I am sitting
on my father's knee. His mother
Farida is standing behind him,
with her friend Regina Mattuck to
her left.

Choueke House Garden View, Autumn

Choueke House Garden View, Winter

Choueke House Garden View, Spring

Choueke House Street View

PART TWO

Halabiyeh in Japan

Fourteen

Kobe Before World War II

Based on my recollections of what I heard from our parents and our Teta, I can mention a few *Halabiyeh* who had lived in Kobe before I was born. For instance, Raymond Harari is a name I remember and I can even identify him in photographs. A generally agreeable feeling on the part of others when talking about him is probably why his memory stays with me. After meeting them abroad as an adult, I realized from old pictures of gatherings at our house that Lily and Isidoro Azrak had passed through Kobe. The same was true of Fortuné (Touneh) Hazan and Adèle Saban, with Lucie all dressed up in kimonos, posing *à la Japonaise*. Albert Chammah, Haim Djemal, Zaki Djemal left before the War hit Japan, as did Nessim and Alice Dwek soon after the birth of their baby boy in 1939. For some reason I recognize Max Hidary in old photographs. Unfortunately for Max, being a U.S. citizen, he was interned in Japan during the war. Moe, his young nephew, resumed the Hidary connection to Japan after the War.

Rahmo Sassoon and his cousin David (Dahude, *Dahudeh*) Sassoon also predated my birth but they stayed on in Japan. Nessim and Esther Tawil together with their children and Esther's mother, brother and sister were in Shioya (a seaside town about 20 minutes by train or car from Kobe). Esther's mother died there soon after the War and the family left for New York. Basha Hazan lived in Shioya until he moved to Tokyo where he died. Murad Attiye (*Attiyeh*) married Leah (*Leechka*) Stolovy, an Ashkenazi girl in Kobe. They moved to Colon, Panama. Dahude, like our parents and grandmother, never left Kobe. He took a long time looking for a bride until he luckily found and married Eliane in Israel and brought her back to Kobe.

Although not Aleppians, Elia and Yael Mizrahi from Jerusalem via Panama were embedded with us and considered an integral part of our tiny community. Elia was our father's bosom buddy and our mother's ideal "farmer"—unpretentious, lively and warm. Yael, Lucie's friend, spoke Ladino and Arabic. She terrified us with her tales of man-eating piranhas in South America! Their daughter, Vicky, left soon after the war. Elia and Yael returned to Panama before Elia settled in Tijuana where their son Solomon had established himself and his family. Albert and Lily Elia and their children also left after the war.

A large number of Iraqi Jews, some via India, others via Iran, were very much a part of our society: The Mattuck family, Sherbanee, Fattal, Victor Kelly, Kelly Hilaly, Victor Moche—and post-war: Aboudi, Bakkash, Wahba, Battat. A handful came to rest with us at the Futatabi cemetery.

Fifteen

Ezra Nasser Passing Through

Ezra Nasser on a journey of discovery
Arrived in Kobe soon after Ezra Chouéké
Brought his bride and mother from Aleppo.

An enchanting lady with a lovely voice,
Newly and unhappily married, eager
And willing to change course,

Found herself attracted to
Ezra N, and he to her—much
To Farida's consternation.

Farida, Ezra N's relative *par
Alliance*, Ezra's mother the sister
Of Farida's brother Ezra's wife.

Concerned for her nephew in-law,
Farida disapprovingly chaperoned
Their meetings in the Chouékés' *salon*.

The timing was off. Ezra N very young,
Not in a position to settle.
The lady, committed.

The beginning of an enduring
Friendship between the two
Cousins-in-law, Ezra and Ezra.

Sixteen

Pre- and Post-War Permanent Residents, Kobe & Tokyo

The Sassoons

The Sassoons were modern, jolly and loved company. Even as a bachelor in his 20s, Rahmo, an active host, threw parties in his nicely appointed pre-war Kobe house, and for the rest of his life he and his wife Renee opened their home to friends and visitors wherever they happened to live. Although we all joined international clubs in Japan, Rahmo blazed a trail for our people by even serving on their boards.

After the War, Rahmo married the young, elegant Renee Silvera in Milano and brought her back to Tokyo where they settled before eventually moving to New York. Rahmo invited his cheerful sister Olga and her equally friendly and caring husband Gaby Josue to come to Japan and move into his house in Kobe. They decided to stay and Gaby bought the house from Rahmo where he and Olga continued the tradition of hospitality. They and their children made our city a better place. Aside from our three Chouékés, Olga and Gaby, along with Maurice Bigio, are the only other born in Aleppo permanent residents in Japan buried in Kobe. And their sons, Salomon and Danny, younger than us, the only other children of our community to be born and grow up in Kobe. They are intimate friends.

Rahmo and Olga's cousins, Dahude and Yaoub also liked people. Dahude spent most of his life in Kobe, amused us and everyone in the foreign community with his provocative and original views. Yaoub, visiting from Turkey, remained unwaveringly affable.

And not to be confused with the other unrelated Sassoons, there were Grace and Cesar Sassoon who came and settled in Japan in the early 1950s. Cesar and Grace, married and living in Egypt, were invited by their uncle Basha Hazan to stay in his house in Shioya while they gave Japan a try. They soon relocated to Tokyo where they lived with their children for decades before they left for New York. We Chouékés adored Grace, this intelligent, original, witty, lovely, stylish lady. We had an automatic hearty response to her. Her husband Cesar, from Egypt of Syrian parentage, was vibrant, energetic and also entertaining.

Seventeen

Rahmo Sassoon

Nicknamed *il Nunu*—
The little one. Because he
Arrived so young in Japan?

Forever in my life, my
Cheeks smart recalling
His painful twisty pinch.

Well into his 90s, still
Smoking cigars, playing
Bridge in Manhattan.

Renee, his younger wife
Endearingly by his side. Until
The end a very lucky man.

A bon vivant, he pursued the good
Life. When asked if he danced,
"Marcher par force," his reply.

And when the same question
Was put to him in Arabic: *Ra'iss?*—
Dancing? *"Meshou b'zore."*

Eighteen

Rahmo and Dahude Sassoon

The aftermath of WWII provided
Incredible opportunities to buy
Properties for very little.

The bachelors with no wives
And families to support put all
The funds they could muster

Into land in bombed out Kobe.
Rahmo then built his Sassoon
Apartments which he rented out

And eventually sold. Dahude held on
Permanently to his undeveloped land.
Cousins, yet complete opposites. Rahmo

Lived as well as he could in the present,
Dahude denied himself, unwilling to sell his
Lots, convinced of their limitless potential.

Nineteen

Dahude Sassoon

Before he died in the early 1990s
Dahude told the visiting Renee Hazan,
"I'm not an 'm' anymore. I'm a 'b.'"

Billionaire, up from millionaire.
He proudly proclaimed he planned
To be richer than Edmond Safra

And he was, for a historical blink
Of an eye, when Japan's economic
Bubble (1986-91) hit ethereal heights.

Dahude liked to tell the story
Of his *meh'sibha*—worry beads.
Nature called while he was airborne.

Inadvertently, it fell in the toilet.
What happened to it? We
Couldn't stop wondering….

When Charlie Sassoon was Bar
Mitzvahed in Tokyo, Dahude sent
Him 10,000 yen (@360 to $1.00),

With a note: "Buy whatever
Your heart desires." I pointed
Out that Charlie's heart's desires

Might exceed 10,000 yen. "What do you
Mean, Sim?" Dahude kept laughing. He
Had no problem making fun of himself.

Having underwritten his nephew Rico's
Ph.D., only to see him jobless upon
Completion: *Fil sikkeh*"—in the street.

He had no respect for education,
Universities, the exorbitant costs
Leading to little or no financial gain.

His often stated expression:
"Money talks, bullshit walks."
Whatever it means…

When he decided to marry,
Dahude travelled the world
To find an appropriate wife.

Finally his searching led him to Eliane.
A better wife no man could have had.
Very sadly, she died too young.

Sitting in mourning for our father,
Dahude felt melancholic, fallible,
Apprehensive about his children.

"You are as young as your youngest,"
(Bina), I quoted a line I had heard.
"Thank you, Sim," he rallied.

For years Dahude had been advised
To write a will. Being Syrian, being
Superstitious, he refused all entreaties.

According to Japanese law, his estate
Was evenly divided among his three
Children. What could be fairer than that?

Twenty

Grace Sassoon

All of us Chouékés loved Grace, this
Extraordinary, brilliant, witty, fun,
And oh so fashionable, special woman.

We could not be happier with our
Interactions in person or by phone.
Luckily I had the most opportunities

To be with Grace, translating for her
In Shioya, visiting in Tokyo, where
Their two sons were born. Mostly,

Later in New York. Ezra called her
Almazeh—a diamond: dazzling,
Shiny and precious. And so she was.

When Grace died in her 90s,
Lucie Chouéké said about her
Very dear friend: "Grace is

Irreplaceable. She was great."
Both of which remain true.
Lucie summed it up for all of us.

Grace Sassoon née Sutton, also
Known as Gracia, Geraz, Garouze.
She preferred Grace. We, Garouze.

Although sunbathing universally
Taken up for the modish tanned look,
Grace differed, thinking for herself.

Smartly intuitive, ahead of her time
She avoided sunshine like the plague.
From youth creamed her face daily,

Radio Cream her favorite. In her 90s
Her flesh firm, unwrinkled; while her
Peers regretted their leathery fallout.

In 2006, before I left for Syria
We had a three hour visit
All in Arabic. It filled the mouth,

Raised our spirits. Please let's
Travel together to Aleppo, I pleaded.
She: "*Hal hleel*"—(whatever it means),

Waving her hand in dismissal.
I wished she would join me
That Lucie, too, could come.

"*Il Surieen kharsaneen,*"—The Syrians
Have turned mute (shut up)—she warned.
"*Ou aideen metrahon*"— and are staying

In their place. My offer quashed,
We spoke of fashion. "Brown
Will never enter my closet," she

Vigorously assured me. I brought her
green tea. "*Ma ba hib ta'im mo*"—I don't
Like the taste. She added two sweeteners.

Grace and Food

Grace and I often prepared meals
Together in New York. She counseled
Wiping dishes and cutlery with a used

Paper napkin before washing them.
That the inner celery stalks taste best.
We made spaghetti sauce with onions,

Fresh tomatoes and julienned carrots.
And once when we were having the
Okra she had cooked, she declared:

"We prefer the small plants." And
I responded: "Who buys big okra?"
We laughed.

I told her about our Teta upset
At the Japanese vendors delivering
Large, tough, inedible *bamyeh*.

Once at a tea party she gave in Tokyo,
I tried her Linzer tartes, the best I ever
Tasted. She was justly proud of them.

For the Eve of 2000, Cesar made
A reservation at Grace's request:
Table à *deux chez La Grenouille.*

She wished for her friend Lucie,
Widowed and alone in Japan,
Depressed with no appetite:

Inshallah—G-d willing, *saha ou*
Afiyeh—health and well-being,
Ou umir il taweel—and long life.

Grace's Sayings, Tales, Expressions

Il arise biji—the groom comes
Ah-la ma kan—all of a sudden
Mit'lil harami—like the thief.

You can judge a marriage,
Whether it's good or bad,
Only after ten years.

Grace said better a
Man with Alzheimer's
Than no man at all.

(She might have had a point,
But not from experience.
Cesar was ever lucid.)

When I complained about
Not understanding my husband
Grace diplomatically told me

"*Tarfi*,"—You know," *il Younaniyeh*
Ben ba'don," the Greeks among
Themselves. Thus she clarified

The inscrutability of ethnic
Societies, relieving me of
Trying to figure them out.

Ba'id il khamseen—After fifty,
Il nomeh kil leleh—sleep each night,
Ma il jahish—is with the donkey.

Bir fos kil mera fi metrah—He kicks
Each time in a (different) place.
(He just keeps poking.)

In all relationships
One way doesn't go
It must be two ways.

When someone hurts you
Don't argue. Just ask for
Two words: "I'm sorry."

A person who puts others down
Does so to raise himself, and
Is complexed and insecure.

Those who preferred and paid
Up for *signatures*—labels,
Lacked confidence in their taste.

A woman upon suffering an insult,
Was advised by Grace: "*Kibbi fil kharej*"
—Throw (it) in the toilet

"*Ou shidi il siphon*"—and pull the
Chain. (Flush it out.) "*Ou la ee him
Mek.*"—And let it not bother you.

Taseh sikhneh taseh berdeh—
A hot basin, a cold basin (of water).
For anyone who runs hot and cold.

Hadi mi'til isit Najeeb—She is like
Najeeb's story. *Takhod ou bit jeeb*—
She takes and she brings (information).

Grace used her own inventions
Hacha bacha—nonsense.
Hal hleel—not worth discussing.

Twenty-One

Cesar Sassoon

Grace's husband, from Egypt of
Syrian parentage. Sophisticated,
Personable, Cesar's ways different

From his wife's, the epitome of an
Ideal Aleppian woman. His Arabic a
Charming Egyptian, his preference for

French, although insisting on the English
Pronunciation of his name. In his later
Years Cesar would say: if he could repeat

One aspect of his life, it would be the part
He spent in Japan. Felt grateful Japan made
Him what he was, where he learned so much.

A devoted husband, father, grandfather,
Cesar remained active, dynamic, engaged
Through to his end in his nineties.

Twenty-Two

Post-War Temporary Residents & Visitors

Just as in our father's time in the 1930s, a second wave of Syrian men came to Kobe and Osaka to export merchandise back to their countries. From New York: Charlie Mamiye's son, Jack; Jack's cousin Jackie Mamiye from San Francisco (dubbed "the sailor man" because he had served in the US Navy); Moe Hidary, the son of Charlie's current partner; very briefly, Alfred Sutton. Raymond Haber's business trip was cut short when he suffered a stroke. He was cared for at the Kaisei Hospital. His wife, Rachel, arrived soon after and stayed with us before she was able to take him back to New York. My mother and I visited them in Brooklyn and were so sorry that Raymond never fully recovered. The bachelors who remained for some years were Isaac (Ike) Hazan, Ezra (Azouri) Sassoon; Solo Dwek; Selmo Haiat; and later, Edmond Esses. Breezing through were Azouri's younger brother David (Touta); and Ike's youngest brother Edgard. Touta was quiet and sensitive. His first languages were French and Italian. Edgard, straight from the Brighton School, had a pleasing English accent and he sparkled with good cheer. Sadly, Edgard, Touta and Selmo died too soon. Since Azouri and Touta were Olga's nephews, they went to the Josues for the Jewish holidays, bringing along their friends. Olga's excellent cuisine, her sunny disposition and her and Gaby's welcoming manner made everyone feel at home.

Renee Sassoon's two brothers, Miro and Maurice were in Tokyo for several years. Soon after their marriage, Miro and his wife Batia, a Silvera related Cohen made their home in New York before moving to Hong Kong and other parts. Maurice married Carol Hedaya whose father was a dear friend of our parents from their ship's stop in Shanghai on their way to Kobe. They spent their early married years in Tokyo before heading to New York.

The bachelors were forever joking. Solo Dwek once telegrammed his father Murad in France from Osaka: "Today is my birthday. Thank you." Azouri, on his return from a trip to Beirut, boasted of a cable he received from a lady he had met there: "*Je pense toujours à toi.*" We were not given follow-up on Murad Dwek's reaction to Solo's reminder, or from Azouri on his response to his smitten conquest. Their nonstop merry making kept us amused.

They all married abroad. Solo to Jeannette Picciotto whom he brought to Kobe, but they didn't remain for long. Azouri married Janie Hazan (Basha's niece) and they also came to Kobe for an even shorter time, also returning to Milano. Selmo and his bride Joyce Dana stayed for a little while. Ike married Rahel in Israel and they were longer in Kobe, then went to New York. Edgard married Brenda Ades Battat in New York where they made their home.

The non-Syrian Elia and Yael's son Ikey and his wife Fortuna settled into the Mizrahi family home near ours. They stayed for a few years, injecting the community with much high spirits before returning to Panama.

Edmond Esses married Fifi Bigio in Beirut. They bought the Mizrahi house and made a life in Kobe where they had their first four children. Fifi's parents, Moise and Sarine Bigio often visited. Sarine, a former classmate and dear friend of Lucie's, and Moise, Ezra's peer, were valuable additions to the community. Fifi, striking, stylish, fluent in French, Arabic, English and Japanese brought back the pre-war allure of our Allepian women in Kobe. She and Edmond with Sarine's help continued the tradition of entertaining friends and travelers alike. Unfortunately, Moise passed away in Kobe. Sarine settled in Panama together with her son Rafael and his wife Frieda, her daughter, also Frieda, and eventually Fifi and Edmond and their families. Their departure created a big loss for our dwindling population.

Theophilo and Yvette (Edmond Esses' sister) Homsany came to Kobe from Panama to which they soon returned. Albert and Selma Dabah with their three girls; and Albert and Frieda Hamway with their three, transplanted long enough from New York for both families to add a fourth "born in Japan" daughter.

Jaqueline, the daughter of Victoria and pre-war visitor Murad Shalam came to Japan with her husband Ralph Aboulafia for some months. They stayed in one of our beachfront houses in Shioya where they met and became close friends with Grace and Cesar Sassoon. This proved the kernel for the partnership that eventually developed between Cesar and Jaqueline's brother John.

Joe Djemal, the son of Ezra Chouéké's dear friend Haron (Rashid) Djemal, married Viviane from Panama (her sister Frieda was the wife of Fifi's brother Rafael) and settled in Kobe. Lucie took credit for the match. Religious and very family oriented as all the Djemals, they had several children before moving to Israel. Joe's brother Maxi came and went from Italy and then married in Brazil. Although much younger, they were respectful and good company for our parents.

Every one of the brides brought back to Japan by the bachelors was nicely brought up, friendly and a credit to her spouse and to our small community which heartily welcomed them all. The same is true of the young couples and families who tried to make a go of it in Kobe. Unfortunately business prospects for foreigners changed. Mammoth Japanese trading firms came to control exports, edging out the entrepreneurs; causing these newer residents to follow alternate paths back in their countries or in new ones.

Our cousin Joseph Choueke (son of *Il Chika*) brought his young Iraqi origin wife Nour on a trip to Kobe before they established themselves in Bangkok. They had to change their Choueke to Chowaiki when they became Thai citizens. The stocking factory he built there was later integrated into his Nasser cousins' factory complex

115

in Manila. In her late teens, the Ashkenazi Vicky Lopata accompanied her husband Simon Guindi to Kobe. They came from Mexico to meet with Konosuke Matsushita, the legendary founder of Panasonic, in neighboring Osaka. Simon, not much older than 20, persuaded the 63 year old chief to let him represent Panasonic in Mexico. Vicky-*chan's* picture took permanent pride of place in our parents' bedroom, alongside those of their children, grandchildren and great grands.

Twenty-Three

Post-War Visitors to Japan

Mamiye and Hidary, partners,
Sent their sons Jack and Moe to Kobe. Our
Sister Frieda vacated her room for them.

Jack bookish, Moe popular, outgoing.
Opposites, with little in common.
Before their fathers split, Moe

Stayed with us for a few months.
Jack spent well over a year, gradually
Decamping to Hong Kong

Where he opened a factory.
Moe, too, more frequently in HK
Bonded with Lucie's brother, Rafoul.

"Steamship" Dwek, contagiously
Bubbly. Did he travel by boat?
Or was it the horn in his deaf ear?

Ezra Mishan, even-tempered, illiterate.
Introduced as the *sensei*—*il mu'alem,*
Impressed the youngsters on the Osaka train.

Yaoub Sassoon, the "producer"
Held out promises of screen tests.
Fun over coffee at the Daimaru *Depato.*

Where did *Jeemie* Betesh get the Jimmy?
American, fulsome, a mouthful
It pleased his Aleppo pals to say it.

Eddie Homsany (Theophilo's brother)
Came from Panama to Osaka on business.
Ezra Chouéké and others took him to lunch

At the restaurant in the Gas Building.
The younger fellows advised Eddie to say
"Jodan" after each order he placed,

Jodan meaning joke in Japanese.
Finally served, he hurried to catch
Up. Sunny by nature, Eddie a star.

Eddie married the pretty Bella
Beyda, a friend I had made in
Beirut, on my way to the U.S.

The most glamorous couple
To touchdown in Kobe:
Doris and Victor Shalom.

Victor served in the US military
Intelligence branch in Italy.
Passing through Egypt, he met

And wed the dazzling
Doris Ades whose family
Hailed from the Sudan.

A love match led to a
Long and happy marriage
For this very attractive pair.

Doris, the Lauren Bacall
To Victor's Humphrey Bogart,
The Shaloms better looking.

Victor and Doris went where
Hardly any Syrians go,
To Great Neck, New York.

Victor's siblings stayed in Brooklyn,
Doris' family landed in Canada. Doris
Told that when the Adeses fled Egypt

During the Nasser regime, her
Mother transformed her diamond
Ring into a hat pin.

How a substantial asset escaped
Detection, helping to underwrite
A new start for the family in Canada.

Leon Hazan hit Kobe
Like a full blown typhoon.
He'd rush in the door

All the while calling out
Yalla ya shabab—
Come on guys.

A fedora tilted on his head
His brown unbuttoned overcoat
Flapping in the breeze,

His face flushed.
The sting of the cool air
Further animating him.

Leon, some twelve years younger
Rallied the late 50s distinguished
Ezra, and the shy, reserved Yaoub.

Ready for adventure they
Responded giggling uncontrollably,
Piling into our big black car.

In Aleppo, long ago, Leon's father
Zaki bought him an *automobile*,
One of four in the entire city.

It became his muse, his greatest
Joy. He never forgot how he drove
It, where, when and with whom.

Behind the wheel of the Buick
Leon in his element, brought
To Kobe the longed for

Aleppo of their youth.
Such bliss cruising around.
Pulse racing thrills exploring

Unfamiliar streets and alleys,
Reliving the ecstasy of
Their unrivalled Aleppo past.

Their favorite outing the
Wholesale food market. The
Japanese with their wares

Spread out on the ground,
Unused to this barrage
Of Middle Eastern bargaining.

No care for the products.
The fun of haggling, the
Excitement in transacting,

Reenacting their tradition,
Dusting off their skills. Although
A pale copy, a reminder of

The vibrant *souk* they missed,
An opportunity to recreate the
Negotiating dance they craved.

Ignoring the spoilage factor,
Returning overloaded with
Crates of fruits and vegetables

To Lucie's and our cook's horror.
The point, the excursion,
Not the trove they brought back.

We thought it very weird when Leon
Called his wife Renee long distance
To ask her what she had eaten.

And then we did, too, finding
It truly intimate. We have all
Become Leon, shunning meat.

Once, Selma Dabbah making her
Way to her hotel room in Japan
Stopped the hall boy to ask:

Is Mr. Hazan a guest here?"
"*Hai okusama*"—Yes, esteemed lady.
"*Doo shiteh wakarimashta?*"—How did

You know? "*Kyuri no niyo'ee*"—The
Smell of cucumber, she answered,
Everyone aware of his favorite foods.

We laughed at how Leon ate but
As we aged, we saw his point. You can't
Go wrong with cucumber, rice and yogurt.

Leon was absolutely classic, what
He said and thought the distilled
Essence of our ancestors. He was us.

Leon mouthed what Lucie Chouéké
Called "*La voix du peuple.*"
Not that it was infallible…

The only instance when he
Veered from our Aleppian norm
Was his preference for brown.

So unusual among our men
Who stuck to navy, gray, black.
We found this rare choice strange

Lesh kil hal bini?—Why all this brown?
Ba hib il lone—I like the color, his reply.
He must have thought it flattered him.

Our father adored Leon
He would say about him
B'ya khod ou b'yahti—

He takes and gives.
And if he can't find a foil
He'll hold up a mirror

And give and take with himself!
His wife Renee laughingly agreed.
When he brought her along to Kobe,

Renee, surprised to see how
Much Dahude had prospered,
Recalled his modest beginning.

The day Dahude left for Japan,
Renee, his neighbor in Aleppo
Offered to carry his pillow to

The station. He promised to
Send her a bicycle from Japan.
And now decades later, on this

Visit to Kobe, she reminded him
Of her good deed and the very
Long delayed reward.

"Forget the bicycle," she exclaimed.
"You can give me an airplane!"
Needless to say she received neither.

While Leon travelled in Asia on business
Renee stayed in Kobe with Ike and Rae
Hazan, made them many Syrian delicacies.

She visited the Chouékés every day.
Ezra happily supplied Renee with
Ingredients unavailable in Kobe.

Ike requested *almaciyeh*—a pudding
Of cornstarch, sugar and *mazaher*—
Rose water. Renee felt ashamed to ask

Ezra for yet another product she
Needed for her cooking. So when
She got up to leave and he asked

Where she was going. "To the
Daimaru." "What for?" Ezra
Wanted to know. "*Mazaher.*"

"*Eh'na Daimaru, shehwaru?*"
—What Daimaru, rubbish? "I'll
Give it to you." Her plan worked.

The Hazans continued on to Tokyo.
Renee, our renowned Syrian cook visited
Our famously *à la mode* Grace Sassoon.

Grace took Renee on a tour of her
House, showed her a room with
Shelves full of cosmetics, mostly creams.

"But where is your pantry?"
Renee asked. Grace answered
"*Mais, c'est ça!*"—But, this is it!

On another occasion Leon
Stopped in Tokyo on business.
Grace invited him to dinner.

She made *mejedera* (rice with
Lentils). Within hours our whole
World had heard the news.

Telephone circuits lit up
Across all time zones as our
People from the Far East to

Europe, the Americas discussed this
Strange and most unusual event.
Why *mejedera*? Such a simple meal...

"It's what he requested," Grace
Answered when confronted. "It's
What I wanted," Leon confirmed.

And where was Cesar? Away.
But their two sons were home.
No one doubted Grace's hospitality,

It was Leon they all derided.
K'teer sa'ub— Very difficult,
They sympathetically concluded.

Leon sent his and Renee's son
To Japan, presumably on business.
He stayed at our house.

His sweetheart Lillian wrote
Him daily numbered letters.
One arrived out of sequence.

Zuki asked our father about it.
"Ana postaji?" Am I a mailman?
Ezra Chouéké quipped in annoyance.

The missing letter never did turn up.
The young couple married in New
York, set up an office in Hong Kong.

Jack Nasser, the much younger
Brother of Lucie's classmate Vicky
Would stop off in Kobe

On his way to and from Manila
Where he and his brothers had
Opened an enormous factory.

Tall, dark, handsome, warm,
A twinkle in his eye, the ideal *Halabi*,
Except for being a vegetarian.

Our house now lonely
Ezra and Lucie urged
Jack to stay with them.

Not to offend Ezra, Jack never
Divulged his highly extravagant
Lodging, an outrageously

Expensive Japanese inn near
Osaka where he could partake of
Vegan meals in a Zen atmosphere.

Lucie referred to Jack as *large*.
"*Roho kbir*"—His soul is big,
Ezra and Lucie would both say.

He brought his stunning new wife
To Kobe, delighting the Chouékés.
A fashion model, tranquil and charming

Ariella won everyone's heart.
My mother and I with Fifi visited
Them in Manila and continued

Our friendship in New York. They
Had three children but most
Unfortunately, Jack died too soon.

Jack would say *"Jar il areeb"*—The close
Neighbor, *"ah'san min akh il b'eed"*—
Better than the brother far away.

Jack disclosed what he liked about
Emotional people: they can't hide
Their feelings, pull off a lie.

Ezra, having confined himself to bed
Gladly received guests in the bedroom.
One day Zaki Djemal from Thailand

Nicknamed *Shoten*—bookshop in
Japanese, he was *zeki*—intelligent.
So original, a maverick, lived in

Bangkok, a vegetarian for 20 years.
He read the encyclopedia. Went with
The flow. Played bridge in Tokyo, and

Like his Djemal family, followed religion
In Milano. Personable, patient, most
Agreeable, married our lovely cousin Frieda.

At Ezra's, he ran into Grace Sassoon from Tokyo.
"Why didn't you marry my sister?" she asked.
"If she was like you, I would have," his reply.

As long as the Djemals owned land
In Kobe, Zakis' nephews Joe and Maxi
came to our city, unfailingly stopping by.

Their bedside presence, first
By Ezra, and then Lucie,
Always welcomed by all.

Our parents, friends of their parents,
Uncles, aunts. We responded to the calm
Of the Djemals, their wry sense of humor.

Like them we were restrained,
Embraced service, felt confidently
Centered, and liked to laugh.

A *Kobe-ko* (child of Kobe), Karina the
Darling firstborn of Fifi and Edmond
Esses with her Syrian Silvera husband,

A credit to his elevated family name,
Sat in Ezra's bedroom, enchanting
All with their quietly joyful company.

Siyahou Chammah was religious
And superstitious. He didn't say
What he would do

Without adding *In Allah rad*—
G-d willing. When taking a trip
He never gave his time of arrival,

Only his time of departure,
Showing total submission
To the will of G-d, believing

He couldn't alter it in any way.
He influenced me. Now I say
I plan to arrive rather than I arrive.

You can't know for sure. Better
To tone down the certainty,
Be humble in the face of fate.

Siyahou had a very strict rule:
No food in the bedroom.
His wife Rahel (together with

Renee Hazan the best cook in
Our community), complained.
Everyone agreed with her and

So did I, until it became my rule,
Which I never break. Ezra, Lucie,
All of us enjoyed Siyahou's visits.

Twenty-Four

With our Syrians Abroad

It was not until we left home that we felt the full impact and the joy of belonging to
our worldwide community. We had been used to hosting our people, now the heartwarming reception proffered to us in turn made us eager to seek out our Syrians
wherever we went. We happily met up with *Halabiyeh* who regaled us with sumptuous
meals in spirited gatherings full of good cheer

> The Mamiyes:
> Frieda and I both received by
> Charlie and Simha Mamiye in their
> Brooklyn home, as their own children.
>
> Frieda learned to cook from Mme
> Mamiye while visiting from the
> Highland Manor boarding school.
>
> I worked for Mamiye Brothers
> The summer of my freshman
> Year in college, as a file clerk
>
> Under the supervision of their
> Patient daughter Molly. Not
> My forté, I probably forever
>
> Ruined their well-kept records.
> Enjoyed lunching with Charlie,
> The intelligent, charismatic boss.
>
> The father of four sons and four
> Daughters, all loved, obeyed and
> Afforded him the deepest respect.
>
> Curious about "kaullege," he had his
> Eldest, Mal drive us to Barnard, trying
> To fathom what it was about.

Teased me about my unconventional
Choice to be educated. Sadly, he
Died soon after.

Through her husband, David Saadeh,
Frieda met and enjoyed the gracious
Hospitality of the noble Abe Sultans.

Unfortunately, Frieda had already left
Home before Leon and Renee Hazan
Started coming to Japan.

I met and saw them there and in N.Y.
Always delighted to be in their company
And that of their caring, fun-loving family.

Along with the Leon Hazans, I was
Affectionately embraced by their relatives:
Renee's mother, Sit Shefia Shalom,

Albert and Peggy, Yaoub and Elsa, Ike and
Rae, dearest Edgard and Brenda Hazan.
The Victor Shaloms, Ezra Nassers, Cesar

Sassoons, Armand Picciottos, John Shalams
Constantly extended invitations and moral
Support, assuaging my homesickness.

On Lucie and Ezra's separate stays in
New York, we were also invited by
The Rahmo Sassoons, Isaac Hedayas,

Joe Michaans, Ezra Mishans, Albert Dabahs,
Solomon Dabahs (Serah, Lucie's special friend),
Cesar Sassoons, Nessim Dwek, and others.

My mother took me on many trips
Where we were graciously and
Generously hosted by everyone.

Starting from the Far East, by Batia
And Miro Silvera in Hong Kong. In
Manila by Nour and Joe Chowaiki,

Julia and Armand Picciotto, Ariella
And Jack Nasser, the Mesries, the
Diwans. We were honored by many in

Milano: our cousins, the Albert Chammahs,
The unrelated Rahel and Siyahou Chammah,
Albert and Fifi Chammah. Azouri and David

Sassoon's parents, their uncle Alfred Shua.
Jeannette and Solo Dwek, Joyce and Selmo Haiat;
Fortuné Hazan, her husband, the close knit Djemals.

Rose and Haim Djemal, Victoria Shalam, Edmond
Safra treated us in Geneva. In Paris Dr. Joseph Dwek;
Alice and Nessim Dwek; Grace and Cesar Sassoon.

We considered Montreal a favorite destination,
Similar to Kobe, with few Aleppians. Rachel and
Leon Safdie, their children, cherished friends.

In Mexico, royally received by our Choueke/
Chowaiki families, Vicky and Simon Guindi,
Esther and Alex Toussier.

Panama mostly taken up with the Kardonskis,
Ashkenaze customers/friends. Lucie reunited
With Vicky Nahmad, her Aleppo school chum.

(Decades later, with my niece Lisa Choueke,
Sarine Bigio, Fifi and Edmond Esses fêted us
In their Coronado and Panama City homes.)

In Buenos Aires, we stayed with Setto, Lucie's
Brother David, his wife Edith and their children.
Adèle Saban, her brother Abou Zo indulged us

With a lavish Argentinian barbecue. The jolly,
Outgoing Murad Shayos entertained us. Arlette,
And her Matalon husband had been to Kobe.

We stayed with Lucie and Moshe Nessim in
Sao Paolo. Emilie and Rahmo Shayo included
Us in their warm circle of relatives and friends.

I am grateful for the universal kindness those in
Our society show one another, engendering in us
A sense of well-being and self-confidence.

It is a privilege to belong to this imperceptible
Percentage of the global population that constitutes
Our unique, very special community.

Twenty-Five

Nassers/Gelmart

Letter to my father, Ezra Chouéké, January 18, 1991

Dear Pappa,

It's been a long time since I've written to you and I'm sorry. I've been busy but it's no excuse. How are you?

I want to tell you about my meeting on Wednesday at Gelmart with the Nassers—not about business but about how really entertaining they are. If you thought it was fun to be in Leon's office and hear everyone shouting about their stocks like *Il Geduh* (the big man), and Moussa and Leon, Albert, etc.…sometimes also *Marioma* Sassoon, well, it's nothing compared to the mood at the Nassers—this is really 100% pure Aleppo-Urfa from the 1900s. I suppose because the Nassers themselves are such characters.

First of all, Albert, Jack and Maurice don't show up until the late morning or early afternoon. They come to this large two story building where there is dust all over, packing crates, desks, offices, everything piled in there. It is the complete opposite of the Sitts at Baby Togs—the Sitts' surroundings are clinical, sterile, like a hospital compared to this *souk* that is the Nassers'—the Sitts are so reserved and formal, you can hear a pin drop. At the Nassers' everyone is speaking loudly and at the same time, no one listens or waits for anyone to finish, everyone is so nervous that while they are talking, they are moving around and you have this group that goes from room to room and through the hallways. Meanwhile, the secretaries and clerks are in the middle of all this, they interrupt with their messages, their ideas. And even though the brothers come in at 11 or after, there are telephone calls from their wives which must be answered.

I had an appointment with Jack at 11. I came on time and there was a man called Nessim Ades already there—we were both given an appointment at the same time! Well, since Jack hadn't arrived, I spoke to this man, he's from Egypt, his two sons work for Gelmart in the accounting department. Later when Jack arrived, Nessim Ades kissed Jack on the cheek and shook his hand and then Jack asked him to go and wait somewhere else while Jack and I had our meeting. Suddenly, another man slid in, kissed Jack's hand and disappeared. It happened so fast, Jack hardly missed a beat. While he and I were talking (I couldn't really talk, he was talking) he was also taking calls, speaking to his secretary, to his assistant and then Maurice came in and sat down. Jack was annoyed because we don't want to stop representing Baby Togs and work exclusively with the Nassers. Maurice changed the subject to where Baby Togs' strengths lie (it's in acrylic knits, according to him). He believes it's impossible to compete with the cheap Chinese children's wear exports to Japan. By the way, when

Mamma and I went to the Gelmart factory in Manila, all the employees we saw loved Maurice. He must be very good hearted. So, while Jack is talking and moving in and out and all around, Maurice is mumbling under his breath: "He should have been a politician." I don't know if he meant it as a complaint or a compliment.

As I was making my way to David Clingo's office to meet with this man who is the head of operations, Albert walked into the building. He had his hat cocked to one side (like Leon likes to do) looking very much like a *sheb* even though he is a grandfather. He was in no hurry to go to his office and it was already close to one o'clock. He wanted to chat with me about you and Mamma, about the Japanese (he thinks they are difficult to work with). He was in no hurry to leave at all. Meanwhile, I was keeping David Clingo waiting. But of course since Albert is the number one boss, I had to listen to him and have him happy and pleased to see me. Actually, I must admit he is good company and a lot of fun.

When I got home, I called Ariella to report to her on the meeting, that it was an amazing experience to be at Gelmart N.Y. for the first time and now I realize why Jack has ulcers. I told her Jack is very creative and that I believe Albert and Maurice understand and respect that. But he has so many ideas, no one can follow through on all of them. At least Albert and Maurice follow some of them. They love each other and although they fight and argue a lot, they really can't live without each other, it's pretty obvious. And that's very nice.

She told me what else goes on and we were laughing. Apparently the brothers had their offices one next to the other on the first floor. It was so dark there, no windows, that Jack moved to the second floor where there are some windows. Well, Albert and Maurice were left alone and would keep coming up to be with Jack. Then Maurice had a falling out with Albert and he moved upstairs. Albert was lonely downstairs so he also moved up eventually—now they want to build another floor on top where they will have a better view and all have their offices there.

Joseph Chowaiki had told me how he eagerly looked forward to coming to N.Y., mainly to spend time at Gelmart. We had the same impressions except that I didn't witness any major disagreements or know about their lunch. So, they all arrive at the office after 11 a.m. They send a fax or two, make some phone calls and then, in Joseph's account, either they have a nice big argument and it is very loud and exciting, or else it's calmer. No matter what, the three of them (plus Joseph when he is there) go to lunch at the same Italian restaurant nearby. They come back and head for Albert's office where he has an espresso machine and makes coffee for them. It is less expensive than the coffee at the restaurant. After the coffee, they go home. Joseph said it was all very "refreshing"!

As you can see, there is hardly any time or thought to their enormous business—some 10,000 people working for them in Manila and the brothers barely appear to be engaged. Also, the people coming and going during the very few hours the brothers are in the office make it even more difficult to concentrate on Gelmart matters. They have to socialize, discuss politics, take calls, serve tea, etc. As for their children, Albert's and Maurice's sons are doing other things and Jack and Ariella's are still very young. This is a gold mine waiting for some energy to be infused into it. Or maybe not... It is certainly successful. It could be that they have the magic formula, that this is a brilliant way to manage and they should just continue as they are even though it seems incredible that anything can get done in such a lively atmosphere.

Pappa, you would have been joyous to be in this place, it's too genuinely Syrian to be true—no Mamiye, Hidary, Sitt, Hazan, no family has this emotional and primitive level of interacting that the Nassers preserved from Syria—it's really, really stimulating. I found it simply unbelievable—the authentic Syrian juice that Grace used to say she had to dip into at least once a year when she would come to N.Y. from Japan. But she never had this experience and there is nothing that can compare with it. Well, bless them, I hope they keep it up. They are a Syrian treasure!

Love,
Simone

Note: Ezra Chouéké died exactly seven months after I wrote this letter. And Jack Nasser a few years after. *Allah ir'hamon.*

135

Twenty-Six

Nassers & Sitts

It astonished me how
We are the same
Yet can be so different.

Their Philippine factories, the
Nassers' office in Queens, the
Sitts' Manhattan headquarters,

Both admirable private enterprises,
Huge successes, yet opposite profiles.
The Nassers' utter chaos, a Syrian *souk*

Transplant: noisy, messy, distracting.
The Sitts': pure order, formal, disciplined,
A superbly run modern business.

Joseph Sitt, the illiterate, extraordinary
Founder, memorized thruway signs to
Drive to his customers.

How did the Sitts create their Empire?
Joseph, sons Eddie and Jack, in-law Sam Dweck?
The Nassers theirs? The mystifying Syrian genius.

Twenty-Seven

Ezra Nasser

Ezra Nasser had an office in the
Empire State building, a fact
More exciting than King Kong.

Just saying it, *Ezra il Nasser*—
Ezra the Nasser, triggers a smile,
Warm feelings, pleasing memories.

When I was a student our mutual
Cousin Albert Choueke took me to his
Office to meet him, the beginning

Of a long and most wonderful
Friendship with him and his wife
Evelyn, beautiful in every way.

He offered help and lent money
To anyone who asked him. Never
Heard he turned anyone down.

There were endless encomiums:
Ma fi mit'lo—there is no one like
him. *Le Prince*—the prince.

Il ra'iss—the leader.
Akhouna—our brother.
Sahibna—our friend.

Il Sheikh—the sheik.
Ras il buhlad—head of the town.
Il Inglizi—The Englishman. Why?

Because in Aleppo, like his *Chika*
Cousins, he studied English and not
French? Or did he carry an umbrella?

Khayer—generous; *adami*—decent.
Eedo maftouha—open-handed.
Albo tayeb—good-hearted.

Witcho dhouki—his face is smiley.
Kibar—distinguished. A gentleman,
Approachable, nonjudgmental.

There was no other more
Ideal *Halabi*—Aleppian, than
The great Ezra Nasser.

When I visited Mr. Nasser in 2000,
He lay pale and tired in his bed.
"We must go to lunch," he wants me

To promise. A poor substitute for
His dear friend, my father. Both Ezras
Loved to lunch, especially together.

We discuss Edmond Safra's horrible
Death the year before. Evelyn joins
Us. We three review the unresolved

Enigma, study the angles, go over
The rumors, the many possibilities.
Ezra trusts the Syrians' opinions.

Twenty-Eight

John Shalam

In the 1960s, when I was at
Barnard, Cesar Sassoon came
To New York; invited me

To meet with John at his
Small one room office way
West in midtown Manhattan.

John sat behind his big desk,
He and Cesar endlessly discussed
Details of their electronics business.

Finally, our late dinner at *Paris Brest*.
This is how I first knew John, observed
His dedication, how hard he worked.

After Wharton, Continental Grain,
Now on his own, an entrepreneur.
The risky, real beginning.

Audiovox grew in leaps and bounds.
John moved his business to L.I.
Fanny, his capable assistant opened

The door for her Cypriot compatriots
To make the trek to Hauppauge. Their
Luck and that of so many others.

John achieved what our wise men
Used as their yardstick for success:
He created the honorable means

For his countless employees to earn
A very good living. Keenly engaged,
They became self-sufficient, rich.

John never boasted of the opportunities
He provided. Too modest to accept tributes
For benefits he bestowed. Always grateful

To America for his chances. At John's side
His wife Jane, the best partner a man could
Wish for. Taking excellent care of him and

Their family, Jane granted John the freedom
To build, develop and prosper. He always
Gives her the credit she deserves.

On the occasion of John Shalam being inducted to the Consumer Electronics Association Hall of Fame, I wrote him the following:

Dear John,

May I add my voice to those honoring you for your remarkable accomplishments?

Rather than reiterate the Western measures of your success—revenues, profits, returns on investment, acquisitions, resourcefulness, going public, etc.—I would like to apply the most significant standard from our Middle Eastern background. As you know, John, in our culture the truly valued member of society, the one esteemed and respected above all others, is the self-made businessman. These are men who, like you, contribute to the greater good by creating jobs and taking responsibility for the livelihoods of the people who work for them, and for their dependents. Judging on this scale, your career has been extraordinary. You have provided numerous individuals with the opportunity to support themselves and their families, and to do so with dignity. Also, I am amazed, especially in this country, that some of them who have been associated with you for decades are still a part of your company or your circle. You have prospered but so have many others lucky enough to cast their lot with yours.

This is why I am deeply impressed with the heartwarming results of your efforts and why I am proud and happy to call you my friend!

With best wishes,

Sincerely,

Simone

Twenty-Nine

In Deal with Renee Hazan

I spent a weekend in the aughts
At Renee's house in Deal. She
Took me to play duplicate bridge.

The Syrian ladies upset me.
So indifferent, cold…until
They heard my Choueke name!

Then effusive, warm, friendly,
I was one of them. Happy they
And happy me.

No longer an outsider, embraced
By *jemait'na*—our people. Swept
Up in the thrill of belonging.

Thirty

We Are Everywhere

> Our far flung exodus from Aleppo,
> Sharply obvious in the many places
> Outside Japan inhabited by our people:
>
> Hong Kong, Taiwan, Manila, Bangkok,
> Tel Aviv, Jerusalem, Beirut, Milano, Lugano,
> Geneva, Paris, Monte Carlo, London, Manchester,
>
> New York, New Jersey, Florida, Washington D.C.,
> Los Angeles, Montreal, Mexico, Panama, Curaçao,
> Sao Paulo, Rio de Janeiro, Buenos Aires, Chile.
>
> I am sure to have missed some locales. But what
> Is certain and memorable, the always wonderful
> Welcome we extend to and receive from each other.

PART THREE

About Us

Thirty-One

Synagogues

Whenever I travel to a new place, I inquire if there is a synagogue and I check it out. I think this is true of all Jewish people. It's an instinctive act, a way to get our bearings, to place ourselves in a new environment by visiting the central focal point of our coreligionists.

Kobe Synagogue

After the war, Rahmo Sassoon
Generously donated the land for
Our small synagogue up the hill

From our house. We spent good, happy
Years at services, holidays and feasts.
Women had chairs in the section behind

The central space occupied by the *bimah*,
With the men sitting or standing around it.
Then one day ultra-religious newcomers

Erected a tightly woven metal screen,
Visually separating the women from the
Rest of the Synagogue. We could barely

Make out anything through the tiny holes.
Lucie felt imprisoned; she stopped attending.
Thankfully, Ezra was spared the sight.

Synagogue in Greece

In Athens Greece on Yom
Kippur 2002. Up a tall, steep,
Rickety staircase, my daughter

And I climbed to the mezzanine.
We sat among many ladies, their
Arms bared, heads uncovered.

Not the self-imposed modesty of
Our Aleppo Arab influence; although
Their ceaseless talking the same.

The men below shushing and
Admonishing the women above
To stop the noise, keep quiet.

Which they would for a few minutes,
Before resuming their chitty chatting.
A universal synagogue experience.

Synagogue in Morocco 2005

With my niece Lisa Choueke Blank,
Our tour visited a very old synagogue.
It seemed abandoned.

On the stairs to the roof for a view
Of the area, we saw a woman
Step out of a door—the furtive,

Dejected looking rabbi's wife.
Avoiding the hostile suspicious guide,
We stealthily put money in her pocket.

The Edmond J. Safra Synagogue, Turnberry, Florida 2015

Renee Hazan, my hostess
Strongly encouraged me to
Join her for Shabbat prayers.

I had no interest but wishing to
Please her, I agreed to go. One
Of the best decisions of my life.

When the Torah was carried and read,
The Aleppo born cantor began to sing
And chant. An irrepressible nostalgia

Shot through my core. Millennia of
Our shared history celebrated in his
Magnificent voice. I asked to buy a

DVD for our mother in Japan.
But recordings were not allowed,
Sacrilegious. What a shame…

I can never forget this most
Spiritually nourishing occasion,
An unexpected visceral reaction

To our devotional words and
And tunes, from Biblical times
Via Spain, Syria and now Florida.

Turnberry, Florida, Email to Lucie Chouéké February 17, 2015

Dear Mamma,

Yesterday morning, Saturday, Renee asked me if I would go to the Safra Synagogue. I understood she wanted me to so of course I agreed. Mimo (Edgard Hazan's sister) was visiting from Chicago and she joined us. The Synagogue is a short walk from Renee's apartment building, right under the overhead highway and facing a canal. The postmodern design (updated traditional) is not like the architecture of the Manhattan Safra Synagogue but it is warm. We were in the women's mezzanine, overlooking the men praying below us. Unfortunately, there was a tall smoked glass screen that blocked our view. We saw well when we stood up for the opening of the sefers.

The cantor, a young fellow born in Syria, was fantastic. He had the perfect voice—beautiful, strong, melodious and joyful—and rhythm for our way of praying. The congregation responded to him perfectly, supporting him, following his direction and not missing a beat. They were all "in the flow." We watched waves of voluminous white tallets topped with black or white kippot, grouping and regrouping without a discordant note. I was never so moved in a house of worship. The unbroken link to our past had such a powerful unexpected effect on me. This was the true sound of our forefathers: pleasing, straightforward, tribal and communal. Members who read from the Torah mentioned a Polissa and a Simontob. If I were a man, I would have bought a reading in Mrs. Ezra Choueke's name. Renee suggested I read along in English but I wanted only to listen. I cared about the continuous historical connection to and the unchanged collective expression of our ancestors. I'm sure this is how it sounded when our great great great grandfathers and all their descendants prayed in their synagogues. I'm glad our Syrians stick together, that they uphold and maintain this heritage.

There must be many members from Latin America because all the announcements were made first in English and then in Spanish. Outside of the synagogue, this mix of so many populations made for an unpatterned atmosphere. I didn't come across anyone who wasn't from somewhere else.

I will write you again tomorrow,
Love,
Simone

Moise Safra Center, Manhattan May 15, 2021

Shabbat at the Moise Safra Synagogue
With Salomon and Karen Josue. Quality
Materials; clean architectural lines.

Excellent understated design; good lighting.
No barriers blocking the women's vision. The
Very able *hazan* chanting our ageless traditions.

Salomon invited to read from the Torah,
A kind and welcoming gesture for a first timer.
An embodiment of our long lasting culture,

The faultless space for our gatherings: quietly
Dignified, elegant, pure, modest. It felt like home.
It is our home. We treated it with respect.

Karen surprised at the seven Cohanim under
Their white tallets; so many for the size of the
Congregation. In Kobe I remember one, Solo Dwek.

Our gratitude to Chella Safra for bringing it
To fruition. I cannot imagine a finer homage
To her late husband, to all our people.

151

Matchmaking

If a girl was *semra*—on the dark side,
"*Suffou*"—List (her attributes).
If fair, nothing more need be said.

Ideal feminine characteristics: light
Skin; big eyes; small nose, mouth and
Teeth. Superior singing voice an asset

Along with cooking skills and wit.
Only one specification for males:
That they be ample providers.

Since we tend to be short,
Women and men preferably
Medium to tall.

For harmony and understanding,
Two classes above or below is
One class too many.

Bridegrooms

A'merji—gambler, the
First trait to beware of.
Be'yarteh—from Beirut,

Hilween bus emfataheen—sweet
(Looking) but worldly. *Il Masarweh*
—the Egyptians, *mahdoumeen*

—Amiable, charming. *Nihneh*
Il Halabiyeh—we the Aleppians,
Rake'zeen—stable (grounded).

Advice to Wives on Husbands

Khali eet mezzmaz burra—let him
Have appetizers outside. *Ou eet*
A'sha fil beit—and dinner at home.

Children

With children, nurture satisfaction,
Feed their needs. Plenty, wholesome
Food; kind, consistent attention.

Referring to boys' restlessness,
Hada kilo bih'leb fihim—this all
Turns to intelligence.

Illnesses

In our Aleppo many died of
Tuberculosis and suffered
From *sikar*—sugar (diabete*s*).

Politics—*Siaseh*

To be avoided at all costs
How to manage? Side with
Benevolent leaders.

Long experience developed
Our aversion to politics. Prefer
Personal relations, aligning

With reputable folk. Aleppo
Influencing our attitude: the
Quran disdains government.

Driving

As in many ethnic groups,
Driving a communal affair.
"Backseat driver" not a

Pejorative. Rather, helpful
Observers contributing,
Staving off lonely chauffeuring.

A carful of *Halabiyeh* directing,
Reading signs, giving warnings,
Not annoying. A whole lot of fun!

Attributes Shunned or Prized

Aino jouaneh—he has a hungry
Eye. Comes from being deprived.
Sheb'aneh—she is full (contented).

His or her hunger satiated, a
Gratified person to be prized.
An unsatisfied one, avoided.

Irritating Behavior

Ha yay bit eed—this female
Repeats. Recognized yet
Exasperating feature.

Meloukhiyeh

Allepians in general
Don't eat *Meloukhiyeh*.
It has a mucusy texture,

Like okra, only more so.
Refer to it as *m'khat*—snot.
Egyptians love it.

Labeling

A woman's traits effaced.
Only one word attaches to her:
Em'kernesheh—wrinkled.

Endearments to a Female

Ya rohi, ya aini—oh my soul,
My eye. Heard so often in her
Youth. Not at all as she ages.

Advantage

Meknat merkaza—she strengthened
Her position. Said of a wife who gives
Birth to one or more sons.

Age Appropriate

Fie sin...—
There is an age...

Attributes

Shay'feh fi halah—
She looks to herself (conceited).
Tikh'jal—she is shy.

The first a negative
The second a positive
Humility over pride.

Jahshay—she's a donkey.
Lazem tir tikeb—
She must be ridden.

Miscellaneous

Na'ah—he selected (found)
Ba'ah—a bug
Da'ah—he touched it.

Al khafif—lightly
Al resmi—formally.
Zit wohra dahrak—

Throw behind your back
(Male). *Mit'il sermaitak il*
A'deemeh—like your old shoe.

Attraction:
Our starkly primitive expression
Be shim min nah—he smells from
Her (takes in her scent).

Thirst can be amorous or not
At'tash tou nah—You (plural)
Made us thirsty (yearn for you).

Reprising warm atmospheres of
Animals in heat; or scorching, waterless
Deserts. Imagined, not experienced.

Ish Akelti?—What did you Eat?:
No need to hesitate. A question
That draws an answer. Keeps
The conversation going.

An intimate inquiry, a metaphor
For closeness, an interest in
The other person.

What she put in her mouth
How she sustains her body
If she is exercising care.

Koto—Chamber pot:
From way way back, a favorite insult.
Hal koto hada—This (male) chamber pot.
The *koto* gone, the reference remains.

Il Ain—The (evil) Eye:
Bit khames—She (hurls) fives.
The essence of the insult her
Shielding herself from your envy.

Refrain from saying five unless
You seek to alienate, showing
Your fear of the other's evil eye.

If forced to use a five add "*Fi ain il
Shitan*"—In the eye of the devil,
Or "*Fi ain il adou,*"—of the enemy,

Deflecting it from your listener.
Or say four and one; or two
Plus three; or six less one.

Mixing Arabic and French:
Zbaleh Française—she's
Garbage, (speaks) French.

My father's generation *Mabrook*—
Blessings (congratulations). My mother's
Mille Mabrook. The French had taken over.

Lat tit felsafi—don't philosophize (female).
Ou lat tah'tini leçons de morale—and
Don't give me lessons on morality.

The first woman: *Inti mit'lil heyt*—
You are like a wall. The second : *Tu
N'est pas raffinée*—You're not refined.

Thirty-Three

Nicknames & Qualifiers

One of the Panama Homsany brothers
Constantly used the phrase *"Sí, cómo no."*
So, *Sí cómo no* he was forever called.

A large, muscular *Halabi*,
They called him *Primo*, after
The boxer Primo Carnera.

Ezra Chouéké named a fellow
Abou Zo—father of taste. We
All knew why. He had none.

Joseph Nasser *"faheem"*—
Intelligent. You never heard
His name without the qualifier.

David Sassoon *"Dahudé."* Tried
So hard to shed the diminutive,
Until he grew old and liked it.

"Harrouloss" from *harr*—agitate
And *talweis*—insinuate. Said
Of a man in constant motion.

Nessim *"Nibol"* Dwek. Never
Could find out what *Nibol* means.
Wish I had asked our father.

Grace Sassoon's uncle in Japan
Always known as Basha Hazan.
Il Basha—the Pasha.

Thirty-Four

Some Family Names

Denoting Colors:
Beit—house of, Azrak—blue.
Beda—white (from *abyad*); Safra—
Yellow (*asfar*); Khedery—green (*akhdar*).
Hamra—red (*ahmar*); *Ashar*—blond, fair.

Trades and Professions:
Beit Khaiat—tailor; Haddad—blacksmith.
Dabah—butcher; Kassab—builder.
Chammah—candle maker; Hazan—cantor.

Biblical Origins:
Shalam; Shalom; Cohen; Levy.

Geographic:
Spanish or Portuguese: Franco,
Laniado, Silvera. Italian: Ancona,
Picciotto. Adjmi—from Iran; Mizrahi
—the East; Mugrabi—North Africa.

A Physical Feature:
Beit Tawil—house of tall.
There is no *Beit Asir*—house
Of short.

Thirty-Five

Female Names

Prior to WWI:
Female names tended to be Arabic.
Farha, Farida, Gemileh, Latifah, Leila,
Naima, Nazira, Selma, Selouh, Senyar,
Setto, Shafia, Simha, Terra, Zerifeh.

After WWI (French Protectorate) :
Adèle, Arlette, Colette, Émilie, Fifi, Fortuné, Henriette,
Huegette, Jeannette, Lucie, Margot, Odette, Renée,
Sarine, Suzanne, Victoria, Yvette, Yvonne.

Thirty-Six

Male Names

First and second born males
Named for their grandfathers.
Their biblical identities unchanged:

Abraham, Dahud, Elia, Ezra, Haim, Haron,
Isak, Issha, Yusuf, Moshe, Salomon, Shaul,
Shaya, Yaoub, Yoshua.

And French as derived from Hebrew:
Albert, Alfred, David, Charles, Édmond,
Édouard, Édgar, Émil, Jacques, Joseph, Léon,
Michel, Moise, Rafael, Raymond, Victor.

Thirty-Seven

Arabic

We are what we speak. To capture our voice, we must hear our words. Arabic is warm, passionate, personal; it sharpens the senses; hot and impetuous rather than cool and deliberative. Our speech softened under French rule; and since our exodus, our language has been influenced by where we landed. Spanish speaking countries bring us back closest to our pre-Aleppian roots.

Arabic, a wide spectrum of feelings.
The countless layers intersecting: sweet
Or fiery love; burning or icy hate.

Worst curses to best flatteries.
The personal "I" reigns supreme
Underlying every thought, action.

Easily warms the blood
Can chill or melt the heart,
Excite, disturb the mind.

Il Arabi be ab'bi il tim—
Arabic fills the mouth.
Just saying it does that.

Ab'bi brings lips together while
Expelling breath, like air
Escaping a sealed container.

Releasing contents, life within,
Desires, emotions, reactions.
Hassisi—sensitive, feeling.

One's energy, force involved.
Arabic words emanate from
The gut; instinctive.

Articulating *"be ab'bi il tim"* requires
Physical exertion for the words,
The expression, the sentiment.

Lips, tongue, larynx,
Lungs, stomach, hands,
All get a workout.

A lot is onomatopoetic.
It sounds like what it is.
An all-inclusive involvement

Necessarily evoking a response:
Laughter, anger, glee, stress. Much
Like Arabic influenced Castilian.

Buh'la hass—without feeling.
You can hear the sensitivity in
The whispering sses.

The saddest word: *il khadah*—
The hurt. Is there anything more
Painful than injustice?

Inkha'daite—I was hurt.
Inkhad—he was hurt.
Inkha'daina—we were hurt.

The sound of a hit—*turr'ah*.
Of a beating—*darbeh*.
And *bosseh*—a kiss.

Bikrah—he hates.
Ash'aneh—she's in love.
Dounyeh—the world (life).

Words for herbs, spices,
Vegetables sounding as
Appetizing as they are.

Millih—salt; *bharat*—allspice.
Urfeh—cinnamon; *ehrinfol*—cloves.
Flehfleh hamra—red pepper.

Toom—garlic; *nah'nah*—mint.
Bassal—onions; *krefiss*-lettuce,
Bah'doones—parsley.

Zeit—oil; *zeitoon*—olives.
Zeit zeitoon—olive oil.
Hadh (m), *haddeh* (f)—hot, spicy.

Evocations:
Ummi—my mother.
 Abi—my father.
Waladi—my child.

Slide straight to the heart.
Jozi—my husband, *merti*—
My wife, don't quite make it.

Sensory Arabic:
Rub'ta—knot; *merboot* (m)—tied.
Ai nai'ha im'bahlaeen—her eyes
Are bulging (she has bulging eyes).

Fa'him il dist—coal of the pot,
(A scarred pot). *Lahmeh*—meat.
Mafroumeh—ground.

Kelb ibn kelb—Dog son of a dog.
Sorer—cruel (m). *Adamiyeh* (f)—Decent.
Im'bahdal (m)—insulting, disrespectful.

Ousouli (m)—correct.
Be shaghel—he works (people) up.
Tishli—she gossips; *be eed*—he repeats.

Bit ajez—she irritates; *be sib*—he curses.
Boom ou be ghar—he is bad and jealous.
Khayreen—they are generous.

Beiton meftouh—their house is open.
Be hibbou il nass—they like people.
Be sah'dou il nass—they help people.

Maa'loubeen—they are turned upside
Down, flipped over (different). *Am bit
De'sha; hibleh*—she's burping; pregnant.

Kilemtain—two words.
Khrabeh—ruin; conjuring
Ghabra—dust.

Em'jalakeh—(she, it) is wrinkled.
Can't you see and feel the ruts and
Grooves in the skin, the fabric?

And one other—*keman wouh'deh*.
M'kinseh—broom and
Keness—to sweep.

You hear the s(s) and the k(s),
Soft and hard detritus
Being swept away.

One fellow confronting another can
Be graphically said to have jumped
In his face—*Nut fi wicho*.

Thirty-Eight

At last, Syria and Aleppo

When I was asked as a child: "What are you?" I automatically responded that I was Syrian Jewish born in Japan, wholeheartedly embracing my heritage. At university I studied Spanish and delighted in the countless words with Arabic origins, a consequence of almost 800 years of Muslim rule beginning with the North African Moors in 711, followed by the enlightened Umayyad caliphate from Syria, crushed by extremist fundamentalists from Africa. Infighting among the Muslim tribes hastened the triumph of the Catholic Reconquista which led to the collapse of Muslim power in 1492, and the forced exodus of all non-Catholics from the country. I was surprised that well over four centuries after our departure from Spain, Spanish words were still sprinkled in our particular Arabic. In 2007 I went to Andalusia, to Cordoba where we believed our forefathers lived, possibly continuously until the 16th century. Somehow I did not feel a tie there.

The year before, in 2006, I visited Syria with a British group. I was on a high before we even landed and never came down from it the whole time we were there. We started in Damascus and slowly worked our way through ancient sites and ruins to arrive in Aleppo, the birthplace of my parents and the many generations of ancestors that preceded them. The landscape was lovely—the desert, the Euphrates and the Orontes rivers, the divine fertile hills and valleys north of Aleppo. And there were hardly any other tourists to intrude on our leisurely access to every part of the country, the amenities and amazing treasures it offered.

In 1999, while traveling in Egypt I developed a fascination for ancient history which, after discovering this part of the cradle of civilization, blossomed into a passion. There is nothing like standing on a tell (a moundlike hill where layers of civilizations lie buried, one over the other, the latest one being on top) and feeling the rumbling energy of combatants stomping in and out of battle; the thrill of walking the ground where armies fought and conquered each other thousands of years ago. Or looking over the Syrian plain of Qadesh, imagining Ramses and his troops up from Egypt in the middle of the thirteenth century BCE, facing the Hittites down from the North; marveling at how, before drawing weapons, both leaders decided to refrain from engaging, declared victory and went back home! Possibly history's first peace treaty.

The six other participants, all British, were congenial and reserved. I used more adjectives in a day than all of them combined in those two and a half weeks we spent together. I found their take on the Middle East amusing: their reaction to the food (lumps of meat); music (ever more moaning); décor (glitzy); the pronunciation (hard to decipher with every p changed to a b—bolice, the boor, Baris, etc.). Lucky for the seven of us we had the tour leader, Jonathan Tubb, to ourselves. An eminent

166

archaeologist and Keeper of the Department of the Ancient Near East at the British Museum, he concentrated on and favored the Bronze Age (3000—1200 BCE) and Iron Age (1200-600 BCE); he had little interest in later periods. When we argued with him regarding the beauty and value of the Hellenic and Roman architecture, he remained adamant that his periods surpassed them aesthetically. We soon became ardent fans of these very active, electrifying early times. Aside from being a brilliant scholar, Jonathan had a terrific wit and embodied the modern T.E. Lawrence type (hero to all British archaeologists). He smoked (including the *nargileh*), drank *araq* and spoke a beautiful, courteous, English-accented Arabic. Fortunately, he never tired of teaching and entertaining us. When we weren't visiting sites or museums or listening to his pre-dinner lectures on history or methodology, we were rolling with laugher at his lightning speed quips and asides. The local guide, Aziz, and Saleh, the driver of our minibus, rounded out our party of ten.

The following is a brief summary of what I consider the highlights of Syria before we reached Aleppo. Damascus had the grand mosque, museums, charming streets full of stores overflowing with colorful merchandise and highly rated restaurants— all together more interesting and pleasant than I had anticipated. I am sorry I didn't have time to look for old prints of the country which I searched for later but couldn't find anywhere else. Even though we were told Aleppo's wares were best, I think for higher quality, I would have preferred the capital. The only Jewish person I came across was someone on a small road in Damascus. He said he came from Boston and appeared disturbed. The last hotel we stayed at in Syria, the old fashioned luxurious Damascus Omayad, outshined the newer Sham Palaces.

Hama had the famous, still functioning waterwheels (*naeura*) on the Orontes River. It reminded me of Osaka—very commercial and bustling. We ate the best falafel on the street there. The Apamea site proved to be a real treat: Hellenic and minimalist in the sublime ancient Greek manner. In Palmyra, our tiny, modest, misnamed (Queen) Zenobia Hotel sat smack in front of the stupendous, enormous, all-encompassing magnificent Roman ruins. Jonathan picked the hotels for their character and not their comforts or modern conveniences. The limited accommodations didn't bother me—the bathroom sink almost in the shower; no room to move around the bed. Everything was to my liking, each moment exciting, stimulating and fun.

Crossing the desert took a long day. We stayed at Deir ez Zor, our hotel rooms look-ing right over the Euphrates (*Il Furat*)—similar to the Nile, a strip of blue traversing the large arid wasteland with lush vegetation on either bank. Of course we visited historic sites everywhere but the ancient ones were sometimes just tells with Jona-than's explanations bringing them to life. We explored Mari and Dura Europos where we were shown the remains of an early CE synagogue. Previously, at the Damascus Museum, we had seen murals depicting biblical scenes which had once graced the walls of this synagogue.

Everyone we talked to would ask where we were from; I never hesitated to say America. Although only speaking in English, I made occasional slips but somehow they were never noticed. I made it my policy to do as much p.r. as possible by not bargaining and tipping heavily. The prices were absurdly low, it would have been ridiculous to bring them down further. They said they asked us our nationality because the Germans and French haggled so much, they doubled their prices when they saw them coming; and the English (referring to everyone from the United Kingdom) didn't spend. They absolutely loved the Americans. Before embarking on this trip, people concerned for my safety had advised me to say I was Canadian. I couldn't do that. It would have been an insult to my country and my hosts to lie. Although we didn't mention religion, many volunteered that they had no prejudices against Christians or Jews. After all, for over 3000 years Syrians had been traders; they were genetically programmed to trade. It was also a prestigious way to earn a living, the Prophet Muhammad himself having been one. It didn't seem to bother them that their ancient sites and museums were empty of tourists since for the majority, history began with Islam. However, they deemed it tragic that hardly any foreigners appeared in their streets, their stores and their *souks*. They needed to expend their energy on business; to interact, persuade and negotiate; to close deals. They achieved self-fulfillment when they made sales.

On one occasion I wanted to buy dates with, as usual, Aziz translating. He warned me I was being overcharged. I gave him my Uncle Rafoul's famous answer: "The fellow has to make a living." When I asked the vendor for his permission to have my picture taken with him and his overflowing boxes of luscious dates, he blushed and turned to the people surrounding us, exclaiming "*Ba stihi*"—I'm shy. I paid for the dates and Aziz took the shot.

We arrived in Aleppo at sunset. I thought I would burst—so emotional to be in a physical environment eerily enveloping me, as if the mist of the centuries of our long past in this exact place continued to exist. It had nothing to do with the reality of this third world city: lots of gray concrete, congested traffic, noise, pollution. Fortunately, the Baron Hotel had hardly changed since 1911 when it was built by members of the same Armenian family who still owned it. To insure their competitive edge, they sagely flaunted memories of T.E. Lawrence—his bill (purportedly unpaid) displayed behind glass in the bar (a hangout for the archeologists working on digs around Aleppo); a large poster of him above the bed in every room. Thus the Baron endured as the only spot in Aleppo where one could imbibe the international/explorer/adventurer scene. Except for the enlarged and updated bathrooms, the rooms remained as they were in our parents' and grandparents' times when newlyweds (those who could afford it) spent their first night here. The management and staff were wonderful—the old man at the desk stocked hand printed stationery and one of a kind postcards. Lucine, the head housekeeper kept the keys and supervised an excellent cleaning every day. Joseph, the slightly wobbly sole waiter, ably kept up with all the breakfast orders, the only meal available for guests. Jonathan, on special terms with the owners, arranged for an Armenian cook to prepare three private dinners for us during our four night stay. While good, these meals and the food we ate throughout our trip did not measure up to the home cooking of our mothers and grandmothers.

We spent our first day exploring Aleppo, half of it at the impressive Citadel. Aziz thrilled to be our guide, this being totally too "modern" for Jonathan. After lunch at one of the many outdoor cafés facing this landmark, we had a free afternoon. Andrew, a young classist fellow participant, and I walked to Sebastian's diagonally across from the Citadel, on a street bordering the *souk*. Jonathan touted it as the best carpet and souvenir shop in Aleppo, an opinion confirmed in publications and by others who recommended it. We met Muhamad Akkam, the 28 year old son of the retired owner. He and his many brothers were given the authority by their father to run this very successful business. Although not the eldest, the outgoing, dynamic, English speaking Muhamad clearly took charge of the whole operation. He had studied in Liverpool and was beguiling in his unusual (for Syria) brusque, direct, no-nonsense way. I picked out one small Persian silk carpet for my mother in her favorite color, blue; and a silk and wool one in coral for my daughter. We understood that if we walked into any store with someone local, the price would be raised 40-50% to cover the commission for this person. Luckily, we were unaccompanied. And yes, for such high priced items I did bargain.

Muhamad then guided Andrew and me through the *souk*. First, at my request, to see his friend who sold photographs and prints (too garish), and then sightseeing: the small Umayyad Mosque; the old hospital for the mentally ill (*Birmaristan Arghan*); *Bab il Gimrog* (customs souk); the *Hattab* (wood), etc. For dinner that night Jonathan chose Il Sissi, an old home with an inner courtyard transformed into a restaurant in Al Jdeideh, the Armenian quarter. With his permission, I phoned and invited Muhamad to join us. Everyone really liked Muhamad, especially with his background in England. We learned from him that new apartments being built near the University of Aleppo sold for millions of dollars! That he was engaged to an American girl who would be coming from Massachusetts to marry him. I am so sorry that I haven't been able to reach Muhamad since the crisis and the horrifying devastation of the country.

The next day we went on an excursion to St. Simeon and Ain Dara in the verdant hills and gorgeously fertile Orontes river valleys north of Aleppo. Ain Dara, a neo-Hittite site (1300-740 BCE), enchanted us with its black, plump, cuddly lions and a temple contemporary and similar to Solomon's. The hills abounded with Kurds. We lunched at a Kurdish restaurant with over-the-top flashy décor. The owner and his waiters had coal black hair, massive mustaches and piercing eyes. They looked fierce.

Back in Aleppo by the early afternoon, Andrew and I headed back to the *souk*. I stopped to buy jasmine perfume to take back as gifts and the vendor was delighted to have a customer. When I paid him exactly what he asked for, he became confused.

"You will pay the full price?" he questioned me, crestfallen I concluded because he hadn't had a chance to enter into a negotiation. I said it was very reasonable (the equivalent of one dollar for each of the small twelve bottles). He thanked me and gave me two extra bottles as well as incalculable happy vibes. He wanted to know where I came from. "America," I said. He enthusiastically responded: "We love Americans! Please tell your friends to come to Syria." I hate to even guess what happened to that fine, honest, and generous young man.

At my request, Jonathan excused me from a day of sightseeing outside the city and arranged for Walid, a man recommended by the Baron's manager to take me around Aleppo. It puzzled me that he only charged $50 for the whole day but I soon understood the logic. When I asked him to take me where I could buy prints of Syria, he called a bookstore in New Aleppo on his cell phone from his dilapidated Chevy and told the woman on the other end of the line he was bringing a customer; and not to forget his commission. Walid was obviously a *delal*—an agent, and would make real money from his cuts. Of course he had no idea I spoke Arabic and it was all I could do to keep from laughing. Later he did the same at a print shop, instructing the owner and his son to be sure to give him his percentage. I wouldn't have minded if he received his share but the pictures, tacky like those of Muhamad's friend in the *souk*, disappointed. Over my objections, Walid insisted we stop at a couple of carpet stores carrying the big ticket items where he could make real money—resulting again in the same failed result for him.

We walked all over, from the Bab il Faraj (the famous clock), to the Jemiliyeh. The population of Aleppo was about three million at the time and the city typical of an overcrowded, dusty, urban environment. Little remained of our parents' and ancestors' Jemiliyeh—the synagogue and the school next to it were both shuttered. Walid could find no one to unlock them for us. The old surviving buildings were mostly empty and decaying. Pretty filigreed ironwork encircled sagging balconies where our women would have spent many hours chatting while they did needle work and observed the street life below. Our mother told us that on hot summer nights, she and her siblings pulled their mattresses onto these balconies to sleep in the cooler open air. The wrecks were just there, waiting to fall down; but could not be bulldozed because they were of historic significance—landmarked but left to crumble.

In the Ismailiyah quarter, around the corner, we saw the St. Louis Hospital in continuous operation since our parents' and grandparents' time. Walid greeted (his) Dr. Antaki, of the same Antaki family of doctors that seem to have served there in the past. The Armenian Jdeideh neighborhood had been reviving—full of renovated old houses with indoor courtyards, many converted into trendy restaurants and boutique hotels. Their jewelry shops flanking these former residences appeared to be prospering. Walid pointed out some stars of David on residential entrances, evidence that Jews had once lived there.

By the end of the day, all I bought were pistachios that Renee Hazan had requested and tapes of Abdel Wahab and Fareed il Atrash, and DVDs of Arabic movies for my mother, plus some spices for American friends. While we made the rounds for these items we passed a bunch of clothing shops for religious women and here, finally, I saw a lot of girls and women entirely attired in black, some completely covered from head to toe including black gloves for their hands. Poor Walid hardly profited from his effort. I did give him a hefty tip to make up for it but surely nothing compared to what he had anticipated.

After Aleppo and an overnight stay at the port city of Latakia, we continued to the fabulous ancient sites of Ebla and Amarit; then the imposing medieval Krak des Chevaliers, one of the best surviving crusader castles in the world. Everywhere we passed, animals—lambs, sheep, cows—roamed freely, eating natural foods. Finally, nearing the end of our journey, we reached Tartous. Sitting in the café next to us, a few brave young girls, identified by Aziz as Christian, uncovered and trendily dressed, smoked *nargilehs*—a shocking sight after the self-effacing black clad Muslim women throughout the rest of the country.

Back in Damascus, just before we left Syria, I went to a post office to mail the letters I had written on the Baron's stationery to my mother, Grace Sassoon and Renee Hazan, who, when she was still Renee Shalom, had been voted *Melkit il Jemal*—Beauty Queen of Aleppo, as reported in the 1946 local newspapers. The ambience of this single story rundown building captivated me: whirling fans hanging from the very high ceiling; the waiting in line; the disheveled clerks in short sleeved cotton shirts sitting on high stools, hunched over the narrow counter spaces between them and us, weighing letters on scales, meting out stamps, proffering change; all somehow exactly as I would have imagined. Having watched the process repeated, there were no surprises at my turn. The shabbiness appealed to me. This holdover post office from our parents' time proved as memorable as the iconic sites.

Notes along the Way

When Syrians say Welcome:
"Welcome" their English workhorse
Please, thank-you, no problem, O.K.
May I have your attention?

Tell Asharine:
Our leader calls it the mad village
On his last visit, dead chickens
Thrown at him. He attributes it to
Frequent intermarriages.

The children:
Sow reeni, sow reeni—
Photograph me. *Ana la wahdi*—me
Alone. *Keman*—again, *keman.*
And so I did.

Brought to mind my grandmothers.
Their uninhibited childhoods
Before the French protectorate
And its restrictive influence.

Deir er Zor:
Watching Syrian T.V.
A male singer
Emotional, sentimental.

With my Syrian hat
I see him attractive,
Feeling, sincere.

With my Western hat,
Unsophisticated, naïve.
How to reconcile the two?

Ebla:
An amiable Syrian guard
Watching over Tell Mardikh
Talking to our archaeologist/leader:

Icecavation—for excavation
Acrobolis—for acropolis
Fortofication—for fortification.

Thirty-Nine

What does it all Mean?

Our Syria, our Aleppo constituted a fortuitous blend of factors that made for an enviable milieu for the many centuries of our stay. The rich and ancient heritage, fertile soil, excellent climate, beautiful topography, the opportunity to trade (before the creation of the Suez Canal disrupted established trading routes, and worldwide economic setbacks further negatively affected business) provided a suitable home for us in which to flourish. Similar elements pervaded our pre-Syrian Andalusian history, some of which Maria Rosa Menocal outlined in her illuminating, uplifting book "Ornament of the World: How Muslims, Jews & Christians Created a Culture of Tolerance in Medieval Spain." We had a social safety net conducive to maintaining our religious beliefs and a harmonious atmosphere in which to thrive. Along with the Christians and the majority Muslim population, we shared a deep sense of honor and respect for others. There were uniform behavioral norms we all followed. It added to our happy state, our love and care for each other, our constructive and supportive attitude which made us want to preserve our community. This attitude has lasted for well over a century since our first fellow Aleppians began emigrating to other countries, near and far.

I think this is why Aleppo was indelibly imprinted in the recollections of our people who knew it and left it. And even of those of us who were neither born nor lived there. I believe it is well worth treasuring our memories of this past and safeguarding what we can of our Sephardic Allepian traditions and values.

The End

Made in the USA
Middletown, DE
30 September 2023

39609161R00106